Silent Witness

SILENT WITNESS

The Story of a Psychic Detective

by Nancy Myer-Czetli and Steve N. Czetli

A BIRCH LANE PRESS BOOK
Published by Carol Publishing Group

A Birch Lane Press Book
Published by Carol Publishing Group
Birch Lane Press is a registered trademark of Carol Communications,
    Inc.
Editorial Offices: 600 Madison Avenue, New York, N.Y. 10022
Sales & Distribution Offices: 120 Enterprise Avenue, Secaucus,
    N.J. 07094
In Canada: Canadian Manda Group, P.O. Box 920, Station U, Toronto,
    Ontario M8Z 5P9
Queries regarding rights and permissions should be addressed to
Carol Publishing Group, 600 Madison Avenue, New York, N.Y. 10022

Carol Publishing Group books are available at special discounts for
bulk purchases, for sales promotions, fund-raising, or educational
purposes. Special editions can be created to specifications. For
details contact: Special Sales Department, Carol Publishing
Group, 120 Enterprise Avenue, Secaucus, N.J. 07094

Manufactured in the United States of America
10 9 8 7 6 5 4 3 2 1

Library of Congress Cataloging-in-Publication Data

Myer-Czetli, Nancy.
    Silent witness : the story of a psychic detective / by Nancy
Myer-Czetli and Steve N. Czetli.
        p.   cm.
    "A Birch Lane Press book."
    ISBN 1-55972-200-2 (hard)
    1. Parapsychology and criminal investigation—United States.
    2. Psychics—United States—Biography.   3. Myer-Czetli, Nancy.
    I. Title.
BF 1045.C7C94 1993
133.8'092—dc20
    [B]   93-23061
                                                       CIP

To the criminal investigation teams I have worked with; the victims' family members; the firemen; search dogs and their handlers, who all gave unstintingly of their time and energy, often with no regard for their personal safety, to bring killers to justice.

Contents

Foreword

A special word of thanks is in order for the brave and open-minded detectives and law enforcement professionals who risked their reputations and sometimes even their jobs to work with me. They were truly pioneers. Back in the 1970s when I was first persuaded to use my psychic abilities in detective work, the officers who associated with me were subject to many levels of hazing and harassment. Fortunately, for most good cops, a healthy sense of humor provided some protection. Many were constantly serenaded with the theme to the *Twilight Zone* or the song "Can You Read My Mind?" from the movie *Superman*. Others were subject to such pranks as finding crystal balls or dead bats left on their desks. It wasn't an easy time. When not subject to outright ridicule, they were constantly hounded to have me pick the next winner at the track or reveal who was having an affair with whom, and a whole host of juvenile stunts.

On top of all of this harassment, some officers were officially reprimanded by their superiors for even working with me. Police departments jealously guard their public reputations and did not want the notoriety of being associated with some "flaky housewife." Some took the time to work with me at home, and almost always had to cover extra expenses out of their own pockets.

Thankfully, times have changed, and some minds have opened. The good work we have all done together has taken much of the stigma out of psychic detective work. With this book we hope to add to a greater understanding of the use and usefulness of a "silent witness."

ACKNOWLEDGMENTS

Nancy and I wish to thank the following former police officers who contributed many hours of their own time to help us recreate the cases in *Silent Witness:* Carl Williams, Greg Sacco, Jay Ingraham, Leroy Landon, Ed Head, Irvin B. Smith, Jack Sines, Jim Moore, Rolf Wysock, Jim Ford, Ted Hawkinson, Ben Ewing, Pete Sheldon, Ray Deputy, David Deputy, and Mr. and Mrs. Paris Mitchell. Also, Kitty Williams, whose remarkable memory helped keep events in the right order and who provided many details on the relationship between the Williamses and Nancy.

Thanks also to William Bonds, William Cilimburg, and Bonnie White, who generously recalled for us, in some detail, tragic and painful events in their lives.

Tracking down former police officers after seventeen years is no easy task, partly because retired police officers, like their working counterparts, tend to have unlisted telephone numbers. Mrs. Bernice Biddle, secretary to the superintendent of the Delaware State Police, and Lisa McNatt, of the personnel office, made calls on our behalf in an effort to connect us with officers Nancy had lost track of.

We are also grateful to Charlotte Walker, director of the News Journal Newspapers library and her staff, who gave us access to press clippings on many of the cases described in the book, and to Katherine Moser, reference librarian at the Wilmington Library, for research on the Aubrey McKay case.

A special thanks to Phyllis and Jess Czetli.

One

Witness on the Water

The morning of July 3, 1975, dawned hot and clear in Atlantic City, New Jersey, as had most of the days of the past two weeks as the trio of Ohio boaters had made their way from Lake Erie via the New York State Barge Canal toward the Intracoastal Waterway and Coral Gables, Florida.

Today was a turning point because when they docked that night, the most dangerous part of the trip would be behind them. By day's end they would have sailed down the coast of New Jersey and into Delaware Bay, up the bay to the Delaware River, and across the Chesapeake and Delaware Canal into the Chesapeake Bay and the Intracoastal Waterway. The treacherous Atlantic Ocean would be behind them.

As usual, Frank Abel, owner of the thirty-four-foot houseboat *Fun House* was up first, preparing for that day's leg of the journey. Lee Cilimburg and Bill Bonds, both nineteen, dragged themselves out of their bunks about 7 A.M. to help get the boat launched, then piled back into bed for a couple more hours of sleep.

As was their habit, the two young men had spent the previous night exploring the day's port city. Atlantic City in 1975 had not yet become the East Coast gambling mecca, but this legendary city with its gameboard streets offered plenty to see and do for two young men from the suburbs of Cleveland.

The trip had made friends of the unlikely pair. Though Lee and Bill were both wrestlers at competing high schools—Bill for Rocky River and Lee for Fair View Heights—and their parents belonged to the same yacht club, they had little in common. After high school Lee had landed a plum job as an oiler on an ore freighter for the Cleveland Cliffs Company and Bill had headed off to Ohio University to study business.

Lee was an outdoorsman. He loved backpacking and had traversed the Appalachian Trail, taking some of his trips in winter. When the opportunity for this voyage arose, he jumped at it, despite his father's reservations.

Looking back, Lee's father, William Cilimburg, has often wondered if the arguments against the trip that kept springing into his mind that summer were logical or rooted in some grim foreboding. For one thing, he worried that Lee would be jeopardizing his job, though Lee explained that he could take a leave of absence. The father pointed out that Lee had been asked only after some older members of the yacht club had accepted, then backed out on Abel.

"Hey, Lee," he had said. "He wants those guys, then he wants you. To hell with this." But his easygoing son wasn't bothered.

Finally, there was transportation home. Abel had offered bus fare. "You have to get back home and back to work," William Cilimburg had argued. "You can't afford to be riding buses around. And if he can't afford to pay your airfare, then don't go."

Lee said he would make up the difference and return by air. In the end, it became clear to the elder Cilimburg just how much the trip meant to his sea-loving son. He relented.

During the day, life on the boat was informal. Whatever needed to be done got done by whoever was free or closest to the job. If one person got tired of steering, somebody else nearby took over in the spacious pilot house on the top deck. The pilot house was a popular gathering spot, thanks to the view through large windows and the comfortable sofa that sat along one wall. At the end of the pleasant room, facing the bow, a heavy steel chair was positioned for the helmsman.

As often as not, that was Frank Abel. A short, stocky man of fifty-five, he made an amiable captain who demanded little of his crew. In fact, by the second week, Bill was beginning to feel guilty about deserting him each evening as he and Lee made their sorties into town.

But Frank was not complaining. So far, things had gone pretty much as planned. Except for one detour because of washed-out locks, one day of drizzle, and an incident in the canal near Schenectady, New York, where they had come uncomfortably close to a barge, it appeared that his goal of transporting his houseboat to his new home in Florida would soon be accomplished.

Now even the worrisome leg in the Atlantic Ocean down the coast of New Jersey was going smoothly. By mid-afternoon the boat turned at Cape May and was heading north up the Delaware Bay toward the canal that would take them into the Chesapeake Bay.

Frank had only one concern. The boat's transmission had developed a slow leak, and periodically he could feel a brief loss of power as the propeller shaft slipped. Adding transmission fluid would temporarily solve the problem. And then there were the storm warnings on the radio. But so far the sky was clear and the bay calm. Frank wasn't worried. The safety of the Chesapeake and Delaware Canal was less than fifty miles away.

Some fifteen miles north and inland, in a residential development called Scottfield, a subdivision of neat, saltbox-style starter houses near Newark, Delaware, a young housewife by the name of Nancy Anderson stood at her kitchen sink, rinsing dishes and placing them in the dishwasher. Within an hour her husband, John, would arrive home from Delaware Technical and Community College, where he taught mathematics, and she would need the dishes for dinner.

From the wading pool placed strategically beneath the kitchen window the squeals of laughter that had been coming from her four- and five-year-old boys suddenly shifted to the familiar pitch that signaled trouble. She glanced out to check on them but found her gaze drawn to the horizon, where a particularly nasty storm had suddenly appeared. For some reason, it frightened her.

She dried her hands, grabbed the latest volume of the *Reader's Digest* condensed books, and headed for the concrete steps that led from the kitchen to the backyard, where she could keep a closer eye on the storm. Hot, thick air and a blinding sun met her at the door. The sky was clear except for the roiling black clouds moving toward her from the Delaware River to the south. Silver slivers of lightning could now be seen slicing to earth.

In the wading pool a few yards away Blake, five, had grabbed up most of the wooden people who lived on the Fisher-Price Happy Houseboat—one of the boy's favorite toys—and now was making a grab for the craft itself. Travis, four, was hunkered down in the shallow water, hugging the houseboat and crying out for his mother.

Blake, seeing Nancy, seized the initiative and cried out, "Mom, Travis won't let me play with the houseboat." Seasoned by his mother's uncanny knack for seeing right through him, Blake didn't wait for justice. He jumped out of the pool, grabbed the garden hose, and let fly with a burst of water that caught Nancy squarely in the chest. Down went the dripping book as she flew after the giggling child in mock pursuit. Travis dumped his houseboat into the pool, where it bobbed among the floating squirt guns and strings of Pop-Pet beads. He joined the chase.

A shattering clap of thunder cut through the laughter and startled Nancy, who was surprised to see how close the storm had gotten. It appeared to be cutting a direct path from the Delaware River straight toward Scottfield. A hot wind began to blow around them. She ordered the children into the house, then ran inside herself to call her neighbor Marty Evans, whose daughter, she had noticed earlier, was playing up the street. By the time she got back to the pool, the wind was sharply cooler and rain was beginning to fall. The air smelled like the sea.

Lightning flashed and thunder rolled in almost continuous peels as she wrestled the heavy plastic pool over, dumping its treasure chest of toys haphazardly on the lawn, and dragged it through the storm cellar door into the basement.

Wind fought her and rain stung her face as she closed the metal shield above her and slid the bolt into place. Flying upstairs to check windows, Nancy was momentarily caught by the view from the triple-wide window in the living room. The trees in the front yard—their trunks nearly a foot in diameter—were bending sharply. The wind seemed to be accelerating, but in an odd circular pattern. Branches and debris swirled on the lawn. Nancy wondered if they were in a tornado.

Lightning slammed into an in-ground pool two houses away and its thunder shook their foundation. The boys, who had been playing in the basement on their Big Wheels, came flying up the stairs. Rain now pounded on the roof like gravel. Travis clung to his mother as the storm raked over the house with a roar like an invisible freight train. Nancy, concerned that one of the straining trees might fall on the house, pried Travis loose and sent both boys back to the basement.

When the storm was over, Nancy walked outside to survey the damage. Branches and leaves littered the lawn. Blades of grass, which only moments ago had been brown, were now green and lush. Individual blades supported large droplets of water. The baked ground had only begun to soak in the rain, leaving shallow puddles throughout the yard.

As she entered the backyard she saw Marty, who thanked her for the warning, explaining that she had barely had time to run down the street and grab her daughter up before the storm hit. Both were impressed by its sudden violence.

From the storm cellar doors that opened onto the backyard Blake's head popped out. Surveying the scene, he shook his head. "What a mess," he said with admiration, then climbed into the yard looking for puddles to stomp. Travis followed, walking out to where the pool had been. He began rescuing his toys. The first one he picked up was the Happy Houseboat, which lay turned on its top, its belly exposed to the July sun, which had once again taken control of the day. Seeing his brother distracted, he began recovering his tiny wooden people before they became scattered and lost in the grass.

Bill Bonds was lying on his bunk reading when, out of the corner of his eye, he caught a dark cloud on the distant horizon. It did not seem worrisome, but a slight uneasiness made Bill toss down his magazine and join Frank in the pilot house.

Lee, who had been lounging on the deck, also saw the storm and joined the other two. They were about five miles from shore, but none of them believed the storm was serious enough to warrant putting in. They would ride it out. Frank turned the boat's square bow directly toward the rising winds and forks of lightning.

Lee and Bill watched from the sofa. Bill was surprised at how quickly the sky went from bright sun to a waxy dome. Thunder rumbled from the distance and the waves grew choppy. The boat began to pitch up and down as rain now raked across the pilot house ceiling and blew across the waves ahead of them like ghostly stalks.

They all felt it when the transmission started slipping. Power for thirty seconds, then a sickening sense of helplessness as the drive shaft slipped and the boat bobbed listlessly in the sea. Then power again.

Frank turned the wheel over to Lee as he and Bill crawled through the howling storm to the stern and added a quart of transmission fluid. Power was restored, but by the time they returned to the pilot house, the storm was raging even more ferociously. Frank took over the wheel again and steered directly into it.

For another ten minutes they plowed forward, as the building waves lifted the heavy boat and dropped it into troughs that were now sometimes as deep as eight feet. The square front of the boat was taking an awful beating. How long, they wondered, could the hull hold up?

Already, parts of the boat were being ripped off. The antenna went, then some of the things they had tied to the railings on the outside of the boat.

None of them felt the *Fun House* could sustain the relentless punishment it was taking much longer, yet there was no sign the storm would soon ease. Waves had climbed to ten feet and the trio had to shout at each other to be heard over the howling winds. Lightning and thunder crashed incessantly; winds whipped around their fragile cabin at more than fifty miles an hour. A fatal decision was made. Maybe, someone said, they should run with the storm. Frank, who had the wheel, began to come about, apparently not thinking of how long it would take to swing a thirty-four-foot houseboat 180 degrees. It took longer than the storm would allow.

When the boat was only halfway through its turn and most vulnerable, a ten-foot wave caught it broadside, lifted it with sickening grace, and dropped it back into the water on its side. Hard.

Lee and Bill, who had been bracing themselves on the couch, were thrown across the cabin. Bill's head went through a window and water poured in.

The next swell turned the houseboat on its top. Suddenly Bill was lodged under the couch. He lost track of Frank and Lee. He sensed that they had moved out of the cabin, aft, probably, trying to get to the dinghy, but he wasn't sure. What he did know was that he was stuck under the heavy couch pinned in a cabin rapidly filling with water. It swirled in around him, cold and salty, rising quickly above his chin, his mouth, his nose. He gulped in air just before it was snatched away by the rising sea which engulfed, then freed him.

The rising water provided enough buoyancy finally to float the sofa. Bill clawed his way to the floor of the overturned cabin, where he found about three inches of air. Gasping, he sucked it in, filling his lungs before diving back, searching frantically for the door out of what his own terror told him was becoming a water-filled coffin.

He never found the door.

The air bubble now gone, he settled to the bottom. Almost from the onset of the storm, he had been containing panic—they all had—trying to keep it caged inside where it would not destroy their chance to survive. They had all managed to maintain some calm—until the boat flipped. That's when their fear broke out and raged inside the cabin like the storm outside. That's when Bill Bonds screamed and thrashed and fought ferociously for his life.

But now, deprived of air, sitting at the bottom of the upturned cabin, he was surrounded by an eerie silence. An inexplicable calm came over him. In that instant, he saw a green light and instinctively moved toward it in slow graceful strokes. It was like a dream. The light grew brighter and brighter, until the silence was suddenly broken by the surface of the water. Howling winds again screamed in his ears; salt spray spit at his face.

Disoriented, he clutched the overturned boat, riding it up ten-foot crests and holding on for his life as it plunged precipitously into deep troughs. It was at the top of one of these rides that through the blackness of the storm he saw lights on the distant shore. They seemed safe but out of reach. He held on, waiting for Lee and Frank to show up in the dinghy.

It was not long before he saw the bow beginning to rise out of the water and realized the boat was going to sink. Bill scrambled to untie one of its bumpers to help him stay afloat. The task, that would normally have taken seconds, took ten minutes. He pushed off and about five minutes later the *Fun House* sank. As it did, the roof ripped off and their belongings littered the water.

Floating with the bumper, Bill remembers trying to salvage their stuff. In particular, he remembers saving a container of deodorant and a yellow sleeping bag that had been lent to him for the trip by a friend.

A half hour after the boat sank, he was still floating around, picking up stuff. As time went by, he absentmindedly started letting it drop away. He kept the sleeping bag and bumper and swam for shore.

By now his mind was beginning to settle down. As his sense returned, so did an awareness of his predicament. Pain stabbed at his attention. He looked down to see blood streaming from cuts and gashes on his feet and legs. Bill reconsidered his escape from the cabin and realized that he must have kicked out a window or at least dragged himself across jagged glass. He had seen the movie *Jaws* the week before. Now all he could say to himself was: "Here I am bleeding in the middle of a saltwater bay."

Panic tried to get out again, but Bill quelled it, stroking methodically toward shore until he felt something brush against his leg. The panic turned to rage. After everything he had been through, some shark was now going to take off his leg. He angrily shot his hand into the water, ready to choke to death whatever had assaulted him. Instead, he came up with a line. Twenty yards down the bay he saw a bobber start moving toward him. His shark was a crab cage.

It seemed like an hour or more before he saw land again. It rose on the horizon at dusk, like a soft, dry, grassy plain rising up from the river's edge. Bill imagined walking up on it and away to safety. The grass was at first two feet high, but as he drew closer it seemed to keep doubling in size. By the time he reached it, the grassy plain had become a marsh thick with reeds that cut like knives and towered over his head.

Night had descended. Exhausted and dazed, he pushed far enough into the marsh to find ground that would support him and crawled into his soaking sleeping bag. He fell asleep immediately, oblivious to the mosquitoes that feasted on his aching body.

It wasn't until Saturday that Nancy learned from a story in the

Wilmington News Journal that a storm not unlike the one that had swept through Scottfield on Thursday had killed at least one boater in a small aluminum craft and perhaps two others who had been aboard a thirty-four-foot houseboat. On Friday, according to the story, a nineteen-year-old by the name of William C. Bonds of Rocky River, Ohio, had been picked up wandering the beach near Route 9 east of Odessa, after spending the night in the marshes. He was pocked with insect bites, dazed, but alive. The fate of his two companions was still unknown.

The story attracted her attention, partly because of her own scrape with what she believed was the same storm. It had been frightening on land; she could easily imagine the horror it had been on the water. A follow-up story on Monday upset her even more. Written by Charles C. Farrell, it detailed the desperate efforts of William Cilimburg to find his son, Lee, one of two men still unaccounted for from the ill-fated houseboat. Bill Cilimburg had flown in that weekend with another son, Ray. He told searchers that Lee, trained as a seaman, must have survived and must be found before he died from exposure.

Most who read the story no doubt dismissed the father's grip on hope as unrealistic. Nancy did not, not entirely.

As she read the article, she experienced deeply the father's loneliness. The depth of his grief bored into her. As it did, images of the floundering houseboat flashed into her mind.

She was inside the pilot house. Two men, one older than the other, stood toward the front as the boat pitched down sharply, then rolled on its side. Both were thrown forward, the older man flung against a steel strut. The other man seemed to disappear from the cabin and Nancy believed he had somehow been thrown out into the sea. That man she knew was Lee Cilimburg.

The older man staggered, dazed and helpless. Nancy pulled back, shaken by her awareness that in her vision, Frank Abel would soon drown.

Lee Cilimburg had gotten away from the boat, but try as she might, she could not be certain that he still survived. Ranging his person-

ality, she felt he had the will and character to fight for life. But it troubled her that when she centered the name in her mind, made him the focus of her attention, she was unable to feel the vibrancy typical of a live thought pattern. Perhaps, she reasoned, he was unconscious.

She was learning more about how her mind worked each day, but even now, two years after she had opened herself to her psychic abilities, her capability exceeded her confidence. Of this much she was certain—the information that came to her in images and sounds or just popped into her mind as awareness was becoming increasingly accurate. The fact both frightened and exhilarated her.

During the search for a missing girl in New Jersey earlier that year, Nancy had accurately described the location of the girl's body. Working from a map, she had pointed to the section of railroad track. The body was later found beside that spur, lying in water just as Nancy had described.

In another case, near Avondale, Pennsylvania, she had been taken to the site of a burned-out house whose owner had disappeared. A Pennsylvania State Police trooper had taken her into the house, where she had picked up a thought pattern. He then followed her curiously as she wandered through the property and into some bramble bushes at the edge of the lawn. At that point she lost track of the missing woman and told police she believed that was the spot where she had died. In fact, unknown to Nancy at the time, the brambles had earlier yielded the woman's watch.

As she was leaving, the trooper, who had seemed puzzled throughout the odd search, smiled knowingly. "I know how you do it," he announced at the car. Nancy looked up with interest.

"You have a finely developed sense of smell, because you followed the same path as the tracking dogs."

"Maybe," Nancy answered, also smiling, "the tracking dogs are using what I'm using."

But what was she using?

As far back as she could reliably remember, as she had moved from country to country following her father's foreign service career to such exotic locales as Ecuador, Chile, Brazil, Afghanistan, and Beirut, she had many times been snatched from disaster by an inner voice that she had grown to trust. As a lonely little girl growing up in foreign countries with transient friends and no permanent culture from which to take her bearings, an inner compass was a handy resource. But Nancy had yet to learn its value. Headstrong and stubborn, she didn't always listen.

That changed as Nancy grew older and came to realize that not everyone had been blessed with so clever a guidance system. Not only did it steer her clear of dangerous people and situations, sometimes it could tell her what was going to happen, though seeing the future was not always easy to handle. Once, when she was sixteen, she was depressed for weeks because she knew that her dog, Samba, would not be allowed to accompany the family to Lashkar Gah, Afghanistan. She had no reason to know this; never before had pets been prohibited from their postings. Not even her parents suspected a problem until it was nearly time to depart and they were told that because of a rabies problem with the native Kuchi dogs, Samba would have to stay behind.

Unable to shield herself with denial, as a girl Nancy was forced to face people's real feelings about her in their raw form, stripped of diplomacy and social tact. It did not leave an adolescent much room in which to find cover.

Another consequence of her acute sensitivity was that she could not turn her back on a task that needed to be done. Her inner voice was persistent in keeping the assignment in front of her and no amount of rationalizing or blocking would get her off the hook. The assignments were not always grand, but she approached them with single-minded commitment. As a housewife and mother in Newark, Delaware, for instance, she helped rally support for the town's first hospital, and to save a century-old tree from a new highway design, and helped in a petition drive to start an Olympic ice skating program at the University of Delaware.

To some, these causes and Nancy's unwavering commitment to her own view made her appear idealistic. Others saw her as self-righteous and even meddlesome. And Nancy always knew with painful clarity how people truly felt. Shy and introspective by nature, she was forced to develop skills to deal with the strong emotions she stirred in people. As she grew older, the fact that people saw her and judged her only by these skills, seeing her as gregarious and outspoken when in fact she was shy and unsure, surprised and dismayed her. Other people, she soon realized, took their bearings from what you did and said, not from how you really were. This awareness emphasized her loneliness.

Loneliness had haunted her childhood, despite a loving and close family, made even closer by their strange and sometimes hostile postings. She had hoped that marriage would ease it, but it did not.

Motherhood came closest but it was slow in coming. For six years miscarriage followed miscarriage. Finally she and John decided to adopt. From working as a volunteer translator at the prenatal clinic for Spanish-speaking mothers at the Wilmington Medical Center, Nancy had learned that while long waiting lists existed for healthy white infants, biracial children were languishing in foster care. She knew what she had to do; the couple immediately set about adopting first one, then a second biracial child.

With her children, she was finally home. They stirred in her new depths of feeling; released within her an outpouring of warmth and caring so strong that she felt fully used, completely needed, and on some level newly understood. She relished each new gesture as it seemed to pop out in her children's play and marveled at their evolving personalities.

As a mother she knew she had to reach out to William Cilimburg. As painful as she knew her involvement would be, not to share with him what she could learn, or help in some other way, was simply intolerable. But how?

She was afraid the Delaware State Police would not take her seriously, but she called anyway. The trooper was polite but indifferent. He listened, he thanked her, and she was quite sure either that he had not written a thing she had told him down or that it had gone directly into the wastebasket.

"Call the paper," John said.

"You know that's going to come across badly," she said.

"Well, it's what you think is right, isn't it?"

It was. She called.

When Charles Farrell came on the phone, Nancy explained who she was and that she understood that people sometimes react badly when psychics volunteer. She assured him she was not looking for publicity. The bottom line, she said, was that Lee Cilimburg might have survived the accident.

How did she know this?

Thought patterns.

Farrell, who was not accustomed to getting news tips based on "thought patterns," put his hand over the phone and consulted his editor. When he returned, he asked how such thought patterns worked.

Nancy explained that with just a name, she was able to describe what people were like.

Farrell asked for an example.

Nancy described his editor.

To his surprise she was certainly close enough. Lee Cilimburg?

"Strong-willed, energetic, and bright," she said. "He wasn't the type of person who would have given up. He would have fought hard to survive. He was also sensitive."

The Cilimburgs, she told him, were very religious "and they have been through this before." Nancy said illness had put one of the children in the family near death in the past.

In fact, Cilimburg had told Farrell that their oldest son, Ray, nearly died with rheumatic fever at the age of ten. In his reporting of the story Farrell had made no mention of Lee's sensitivity, nor had he detailed much about the family, certainly not Ray's bout with rheumatic fever. Nothing was rock solid, but Farrell was becoming intrigued. He picked Nancy up and accompanied her to the Bay View and Augustine Wildlife areas, which were close to where Nancy believed the boat had sunk. Nancy felt that if she got closer to the scene of the accident, she might learn more.

As Farrell wrote in a story that appeared the following Friday, she "gazed silently into the Delaware River, as if seeking a message from the waters."

And that was precisely what she had been doing. Standing on the shore at the Augustine Wildlife Area, once again centering Lee Cilimburg in her attention, she found herself above a wind-crazed sea of giant swells, swimming alongside Lee Cilimburg as he struggled to survive.

He is swimming, but he has no idea what direction he is swimming in. He can't see anything. He tries to stay cool. He is tough. He is going to beat it. And he is fine, until a cable or chain gets tangled in his left leg and pulls him under.

She said softly to Farrell, "I don't think he made it."

Her break with the river was abrupt. She turned, hoping to cut herself off from the sadness that had streamed into her with the tragic vision of Lee. But while the images evaporated, the sadness stayed. As she walked back toward Farrell's compact car, he asked if she was all right.

She nodded. He waited a moment, then asked if she knew where or when the bodies would wash up.

Nancy said that Frank Abel would be found that day. (In fact Farrell already knew—but had been restrained from releasing the fact—that a body believed to be that of Abel had been pulled from the Delaware River channel earlier that day.)

He asked when Lee would be found and she said probably Wednesday.

Where?

Nancy shrugged. Farrell asked if a map would help.

"Maybe," she said.

He unfolded a Delaware State road map on the hood of his car. As Farrell smoothed the wrinkles out of it, Nancy's hand shot out and pointed to the mouth of the Appoquinimink River. She couldn't pronounce it, but she knew that was the place.

As Farrell drove her back to Newark, Nancy stared out the side window, shaken and dejected. Until the moment by the river she had truly believed Lee might have survived. Confronted with his death, she just wanted to go home. There was nothing more she felt she could do.

William Cilimburg felt otherwise.

Port Penn has one stoplight, which made it easy for Lee's father to recognize Nancy's VW bug as it scooted down Route 9 and came to a halt in the middle of town.

When he emerged from his car and started to trudge toward her, Nancy judged him to be only slightly taller than her own five feet nine inches. He wore simple blue walking shorts and a tank top, and days of searching the river for his son had turned his skin a beet red. The brim of a cap cast a shadow over his eyes. He walked with purpose, but there was despair in his face.

She had called him reluctantly at Farrell's suggestion the night before. The reporter had said Cilimburg wanted to talk. Before, she had been anxious to share her hope with him. Now, she dreaded the encounter.

Cilimburg did not know what to expect when he approached Nancy. He was at his wit's end for new leads and the hope that had sustained him was beginning to disappear. The day before, seeing what the river had done to Frank Abel had not helped.

Police had asked him to make a positive identification at the morgue in Wilmington. When he walked into the room where the corpse was stored, he was not ready for what he saw.

"You apparently got the wrong guy, because that's obviously a black man and he must weight three hundred pounds," Cilimburg said.

"No, that's a white man, five-foot-eight, that weighs about one hundred sixty pounds," he was told.

But while police had failed to warn him about the condition of a corpse after four days in the water, they did warn him about psychics, who, they said, sometimes exploit tragedies like this for publicity and fees.

So when he leaned over to talk to Nancy through her car window, he was torn between wariness and desperation.

Nancy recalls his piercing blue eyes and kind, weathered face, creased with worry and sadness. She agreed to take him to the spot where she and Farrell had stood the day before. Ray and Lee's uncle stayed in the car while Nancy and Lee's father walked the three hundred feet to the river's edge and sat on a picnic bench.

Nancy reviewed her version of events. It was one of the hardest things she had ever done.

"He fought hard, even after he got tangled," she concluded. "He was a very strong boy who didn't give up. He was very brave." But she knew even as she said the words that they would be of little comfort to Lee's father.

At points during her description, he would become choked with emotion and shake his head. Unable to speak without sobbing, he would stop, compose himself, then continue.

Nancy waited. The father withdrew from his well-worn wallet a picture of Lee and handed it to her, as if to introduce him. She gazed down at what appeared to be a high school graduation picture of a vital, handsome man with his father's eyes and thick blond hair. Nancy felt that Lee's father was hoping the picture would bring other visions—visions with happier endings. But it did not. Holding it between her hands, she talked about Lee, about what he was like. His father remembers that what she told him that day was accurate; he could no longer doubt that she was somehow connected with his lost son.

"I just can't accept that he's dead," Cilimburg said when she was finished.

"I understand that," Nancy said. "With my own two sons, until I had to confront it directly, I'd feel the same way."

"To give you a description of him, he was so kind to animals, he would never step on an ant," the father said. "I said, 'For chrissakes, there's millions of them.' He said, 'It don't matter.

Everything is living. You don't step on it.' He wouldn't."

Cilimburg turned and walked slowly along the river's edge. Nancy let him go.

When she turned around, she found that Lee's brother Ray had gotten out of the car and made his way to the picnic table. He had been listening, but she was so intent on consoling the elder Cilimburg she had not noticed.

"I want it not to be true, but inside I think Lee's dead too," he said. "I don't know what I'm going to do, because when we have to face this, I don't think my dad is going to be able to handle it."

When they had been introduced, she had been struck immediately by Ray's sensitivity. Unlike his brother. who was squarely built, Ray was thin with broad shoulders. He had an almost ascetic look.

"Your dad is a brave man and he will handle it," Nancy told him. She counseled him on what to expect from different members of his family, how they would react. The fact that Nancy seemed to know specific members of his family so well somehow seemed to make Ray feel less bereaved, if only for a moment.

When the elder Cilimburg returned, they retrieved some maritime charts from his car and Nancy attempted to locate the site of the accident. She had always found maritime charts indecipherable, so trying to read them was pointless. Instead, she rubbed her hand lightly over the surface of each section map until she felt warmth. "There," she said, "that's where the boat went down." It was the same location she had pointed out to Farrell the day before.

There seemed little more she could do for these people. The conversation tailed off, yet she hated to leave. Their emptiness ached in her. She wanted to crush them all in a huge embrace.

Instead, they walked back to their cars in silence. Bill Cilimburg asked Nancy if he could buy her lunch.

No, she said, she had to get back home to relieve the baby-sitter.

Could he pay for the sitter?

No.

Could he put gas in her car?

No.

They thanked her for her help, but the elder Cilimburg could not help but add that he hoped she was wrong.

"Well, quite frankly, I do too," said Nancy. "I hope we find him wandering around out in the swamps somewhere."

But she knew they would not.

Lee Cilimburg's body was found that Thursday morning about three hundred yards offshore near the mouth of the Appo-quinimink River by an ecology group doing research. Nancy had called the spot and was only hours off on the time. Missing from the body were glasses, without which, Lee's father had said, his son was virtually blind—a possible explanation for the disorientation Nancy reported.

When William Cilimburg came to Wilmington to identify his son, he asked the coroner if there had been any indication that a cable or chain had tangled with his boy's legs. He was told that there appeared to be marks on the left leg that suggested it had been wrapped in some sort of cable.

Two

Fly, Robin, Fly

The Delaware State policeman who banged on Nancy Anderson's door that May afternoon in 1976 was a solidly built man of average height with black hair and piercing hazel eyes. His manner was abrupt and indifferent. He would bang on the door, then turn to his partner with a half laugh and shake his head.

To Detective Carl Williams, this visit to a fortune-teller in Newark was a joke. Williams liked a good joke, but *God*, he hated to waste time. That was clear from the closure record he had achieved in the few short months since he had been handpicked by Col. Irvin B. Smith, superintendent of the Delaware State Police, to run a special investigative unit. Its job was to close cases other detectives could not. Most were cold—a year or more old. But Williams and his troop of half a dozen or so maverick detectives were closing them at a record clip.

His success did not make him popular, but then Williams never did too well in popularity contests anyway. Too honest, he told himself, too direct. Now he could add jealousy, although the one-word explanations sometimes nagged at him as too easy.

His assignments came directly from Smith, who was known alternately as the colonel or Smitty, depending upon one's rank or fondness for formality. Williams called him Smitty.

"You got a new case," Smith announced. Williams waited for the explanation. "Every time I stop in for gas at this little station on Route Thirteen, I get an earful about what the hell good are the state police when they can't solve a gas station robbery. A kid is in a coma at A. I. Du Pont Hospital. I want you to talk to him."

Williams was suddenly confused. "Talk to who?"

"The victim."

"I thought you said he was in a coma."

"I did."

"How the hell am I going to talk to him if he's in a coma?"

Smith didn't say anything.

"And why do I need to talk to him, even if I could? I'll pick up the report like I always do," Williams said.

"No," Smith said, "I'm going to send this girl up with you, and I want you to take her with you and you go in and talk to him."

Williams was beginning to tumble to the nature of the next day's interrogation. "What girl?"

"Nancy Anderson," Smith replied. "Remember Cilimburg? She picked the day and spot the boy would float up. She has a gift."

"Excuse me?"

"She knows things." "She can help us get the job done."

Getting the job done was Smith's favorite phrase. It could have been the slogan of his administration.

"Maybe she can help *you*, but I'm not taking her," Williams responded. "I don't believe in that voodoo shit. You take her."

There was a short silence, then the colonel's baritone voice slowly intoned, "Sergeant..." Williams knew he was wasting time arguing.

"Okay, I'll take her, but I'm not going to be nice," he said. "I'm taking her up, I'm bringing her back, and that's the end of that shit."

It was clear to Nancy as she peered out her wide living room window that the man striding up to her front porch wanted to be anywhere but at her door that brilliant spring day. The insight did little to ease her own misgivings about this experiment. In fact, it made her mad that she had not stuck by her guns and refused to be worn down by Colonel Smith's marathon campaign—what he called "polite police harassment." In truth, despite accurate work she had done for families in New Jersey and Pennsylvania, she was still not convinced psychic impressions were specific or consistent enough for police work.

The publicity surrounding her stunning predictions in the Cilimburg boating accident had briefly made her a local celebrity. It had also created towering expectations. Now she was being asked to do police work and she wasn't at all sure she could get it right.

And what if she did, even occasionally? She would have to put herself through the same emotional trauma as the victim. What if she screwed up? She didn't need the ridicule or the pressure. The idea of hundreds of police officers spending thousands of man-hours chasing clues she dragged out of her imagination terrified her. She even fantasized that if she got it wrong, she might be arrested; or if she got it too right, she might be a suspect.

But the colonel was an impressive man. He stood bolt upright, a military posture that gave him instant authority. When he spoke, it was in a resonant voice that was so confident and natural, it would rarely occur to a listener to doubt or disobey.

Nancy also had to admit to herself that his attempts to recruit her were flattering.

She had first encountered Irvin Smith at a seminar she had given at Delaware Technical and Community College more than two years before. He had been assigned by then-superintendent James Ford to see if the training in intuition that Nancy's seminar promised could be useful in police work. Smith was personally curious to find out if what the police liked to call "the luck of the draw" might be something other than coincidence.

Nancy did psychometry that day, demonstrating the ability to discern information from inanimate objects. Among the objects she held was Smith's police academy ring. The detail and accuracy of what she said left an indelible impression on him. Among her comments was the prediction that he would come to be in command of men.

Two years later Smith was indeed in command of men. He had been appointed superintendent of the Delaware State Police, a position that put him in charge of more than 470 officers in nine troops from Wilmington to Georgetown. It was late winter of 1976 when their paths crossed again at the Dupont Country Club in Wilmington. Nancy was once more demonstrating her ability to read people through objects that were emotionally important to them, but Capt. Pete "Bones" Sheldon, a close friend of Smith's, was having none of it.

Sheldon's nickname came from his gangly frame and craggy face. At six-four, he towered over most other men, but his view of police procedure was decidedly down-to-earth. He called it "hardnosed and down the line" and it did not include pretty ladies "standing off to the side feeling a sock or shirt and saying this is what happened."

Sheldon and Smith were close enough friends for the captain to get away with tweaking the colonel's odd belief in most anything, certainly something as nonstandard as this Newark housewife. Both men were ex-marines who had joined the state police about the same time. The night Smith got word of his promotion to colonel, it was Sheldon's house he visited with his wife and a bottle of wine.

"Aw, I can't buy this, man," Sheldon was saying to Smith, shaking his head as if to free it of his friend's cockeyed notion. "There is just no way."

"Bones," Smith said, "I'm telling you flat-out I had never met the lady before and she told me things about myself and my family that only my family and I know."

Drawn by the intensity of their conversation, Nancy asked if Sheldon would volunteer an object that was important to him. He started to shake her off but stopped suddenly and pulled out his wallet. It did not take Nancy long to understand the turnaround in Sheldon's attitude. Though warm from his body, the black leather billfold was emotionally cold.

"This is no good," she said.

Sheldon let his grin grow as he looked at Smith. "See?"

"Wait a minute, just wait a minute," Smith said.

Nancy continued. "This is a new wallet. You haven't had this wallet very long."

Sheldon looked stricken. In fact, he had only purchased it six weeks before. Ducking his head, he reached to retrieve it.

"I have to have something that you've had for a good while and that you feel close to," Nancy repeated. "Something that has a lot of sentimental value to you."

Embarrassed, Sheldon reluctantly handed her his watch.

She held it for a minute, then looked directly at him. "I don't want to talk to you about this right now, but you are having personal problems with one of your sons, and if you want to talk to me, we can talk after the meeting, but not now." She went on to tell Sheldon less sensitive facts about himself, his family and his past, things that she would have had no normal way of knowing.

Sheldon was stunned. In fact, he *was* having trouble with one of his older sons and the rest of the information about him was right on.

It was the next day that Smith called.

That day and every other weekday for the next nine weeks.

"Nancy," he would say, "I have some cases I really think you could help us on. Just come over for lunch. We'll take you over to the academy and get you something to eat and we can talk these cases over."

And she would reply, "I've got a lot I'm thinking about. I've got a lot on my mind. That's not what I've got on my mind now."

Smith was polite and low-key, but he always ended the conversation by saying that he would just have to work harder to persuade her.

Eventually she got the message: the phone calls would only stop when she proved to Smith that psychic information was not precise enough to be useful in police work.

"Okay," Colonel Smith had said, "You go ahead and show me. And if you are right, I'll apologize and take you to lunch and it will all be over with."

Even as she agreed, she was planning on dragging her heels, but Smith was ready.

"When can we set that up?" he asked.

Nancy winced. She liked it better when she was the one reading minds.

"I don't know, I have to make arrangements for the kids," she said.

"Okay," said Smith. "You make arrangements and call me back."

Of course, she didn't, but he did and this time she committed to a date. A week later, Carl Williams came knocking on her door.

He was dressed in an ordinary business suit, but to Nancy there was no mistaking this man's calling. And that's the word she would use, *calling*. Police work was his life, an obsession with him. She also knew that this was the last place he wanted to be on this brilliant spring day.

"Carl Williams, Delaware State Police," he said in a bored monotone. "Colonel Smith sent us to pick up a Nancy..." He feigned a puzzled look as he turned to the man behind him.

"Anderson," said his partner, seeming embarrassed by his boss's sudden memory loss. Then he introduced himself.

"Greg Sacco," he said. He was taller and younger than Williams and in a markedly better mood.

Nancy stooped to grab her barking beagle by the collar and twisted to open the door with her free hand. As the men entered, she found herself in an awkward posture, gazing up and sideways into the impatient glare of Williams.

"I'm Nancy Anderson," she said, struggling with the lunging beagle. Realizing how ridiculous she looked and that the door was now closed, she let go of the collar. Although the beagle had the demeanor of a Doberman when restrained, set free he seemed at a loss. He cast a puzzled look up at Nancy, then trotted over to Sacco and ran his nose up and down the man's trouser legs. Satisfied, he stretched and put his paws on Sacco's knees. The junior officer rubbed the dog's head and asked Nancy his name.

"George," she said.

Williams rolled his eyes toward the ceiling and moved further into the living room, where he could see more of the place. Sacco and Nancy followed, George trailing behind. For a moment they all just stood there awkwardly, not knowing quite what to do.

"Colonel Smith wants you to talk to a boy at A. I. Du Pont Hospital," Williams finally said. "Only the boy is in a coma. Any idea how you're going to do that?"

"No," Nancy said. "I've only worked on police cases a couple of times. I told Colonel Smith that. This wasn't my idea."

"It wasn't my idea either," Williams said.

Nancy had expected skepticism, even a mechanical indifference. A polite, stony-faced trooper going through the motions. She was not prepared for Williams.

They stared at each other for a while and finally she said, "I'll tell you what. I don't think it will work either. This is Colonel Smith's idea. He has been calling me on the phone for nine solid weeks and this is the only way I'm going to get rid of him. I'm going to go out and show him it won't work and then we'll both be rid of this problem."

Sure, Williams thought, but he did his best to stifle the reaction. It wasn't easy. His attitude had a way of showing on his face. It was a problem that had plagued him since his school days. He had forever been in trouble with teachers and his defense had always been the same: "What did I say? I didn't say anything."

And the teachers would say, "You don't have to say anything."

And Williams would think, *I have to learn to mask my thoughts.*

George had followed them into the living room and now was circling Williams, warily trying to get close enough to smell him. Williams cast him a withering look and George retreated to his favorite chair.

Sacco broke the silence. "How about we go down to Dover first?"

Dover was an arson site. It was also more than an hour's drive south and among the things Williams had been trying to figure out on the way over was how they could keep Smitty off their back and save the drive and the time. Although he didn't believe another person could actually read your thoughts, neither did he savor the idea of being locked up in a car for an hour with a housewife who thought she could.

"Why don't you just show her the pictures?" he said to Sacco. Sacco looked at Nancy, who shrugged.

"I just don't know," she said. "It might help to be at the site."

"Why don't we take her down?" Sacco said.

"Why don't we," Williams echoed.

The ride to the state capital seemed long and lonely to Nancy, who sat in the backseat, mostly ignored.

As they drove, Sacco occasionally took a stab at small talk, kids mostly. Nancy told the story of Blake's getting wedged in his bunk bed by jumping up and down as if it were a trampoline. On one unlucky descent, his feet slipped between the side of the steel box spring and the bed frame and he came to rest embedded neatly up to his waist. Try as she might, Nancy couldn't budge him. Travis had had to keep feeding him chocolate chip cookies to keep him calm so he wouldn't sink any further while they waited for the rescue squad. The cookies worked too, until he saw a red-suited fire fighter stride into his bedroom with the Jaws of Life and thought they were going to have to cut him apart to get him out. As it turned out, all that was needed was a strong push on the box spring from below.

Nancy thought she saw in the rearview mirror a fleeting smile scamper across the driver's face, but she couldn't be sure. She decided Williams must have children.

"You worked on that houseboat accident, didn't you?" Sacco said. It was clear to her that it wasn't as much a question as a statement.

"I talked to a reporter for the *News Journal* and he contacted the family," she said. "I called Troop 6 and told them what I knew, but the officer didn't take me seriously."

"Probably put it in the circular file," Williams said. "I would have."

"Is that for drowning victims?" Nancy asked. Her years overseas had resulted in some language gaps, especially colloquialisms.

"You picked the location of the boy's body and when it would be found, I think, didn't you?" Sacco quickly interjected.

"It was sad. The father was so sure his son was too good a seaman to have drowned, and to be honest, I thought he might have survived until the day I went down to the edge of the river with the reporter. Then I knew."

"How did you know?" Sacco asked.

"I saw it," Nancy said.

"You saw it." Williams repeated, his voice flat.

"In my mind, I saw what happened. It was like a movie, only I wasn't watching it as much as reliving it."

Williams cast a baleful glance at Sacco for bringing the subject up, but his partner's curiosity would not be squelched.

"How do you do that?" Sacco asked.

Nancy thought for a moment. Sometimes she felt more like it was done to her than the other way around. *How did she do it? It was almost the opposite of making an effort, and yet she was guiding it.* Although she had some ideas, she didn't feel like exploring them in such hostile company. She finally settled on, "I'm not sure."

Finally they pulled off the road into a large parking lot surrounding a sprawling warehouse and office complex that seemed to sprout from the fields that lay just outside the city of Dover itself. They circled the building several times. After three circuits, Williams braked to a stop near the entrance and shifted into park. He twisted around in his seat and glared at her.

"Well?" he said.

"Oh," Nancy said. "I thought you were going to take me to a burned-out building." As soon as the words tumbled out, she was sorry. *Great psychic,* she was sure Williams was thinking.

Nancy's stomach churned and tightened. She struggled to stay calm, because whatever she did, she knew it was necessary to be calm and centered. Imagining the blast she was going to level at Colonel Smith helped.

Williams tried to exchange looks with Sacco, but Sacco refused to catch his eyes. Looking at Nancy, Sacco asked, "Can you work from this? I have the file here; do you want to look at the photos?" He squeezed a large accordion file out from between his feet.

"No, just let me use the scene initially and maybe I'll look at the photos afterward."

It was growing warm in the car. Nancy unbuttoned her jacket and leaned against the window. Williams put the car back in gear and started slowly around the building one last time. The motion helped Nancy relax, relax and focus.

Without warning she was inside a barn. It was the last thing she had expected, but the pungent scent of moist hay and mildew was unmistakable. She had been inside too many barns with her dad not to recognize the setting, yet something in her vision was off. She looked around. There was very little light, only the scent of…gasoline? Where were the animals? Where was the smell of manure? In the dimly lit structure, she sensed vague outlines of what seemed to be machinery. What kind of machinery? With the question came an image of a John Deere symbol and then a tractor, several tractors, a combine with its huge paddlewheel-like maw. Other farm machinery popped into view. And then among the farm machines was a tank truck. Odd, she thought. Its spigot was open and a tan liquid danced onto the barn's cement floor and flowed toward a tarpaulin spread between pieces of equipment.

Two men moved methodically among the tractors. She could see them quite well, which didn't make sense in the darkened barn. One carried a can; the other held a fistful of candles. She watched in silence as they unhurriedly placed the cans and candles on the tarpaulin.

"Got enough vibes yet?"

Williams's distinctive voice pulled her instantly out of the scene and back into the car. The intrusion annoyed her.

"Yes, Sergeant Williams," she said. "I think I have enough vibes."

The detailed vision built her confidence but also worried her. *You could actually identify somebody from the pictures you're getting in your head,* she thought. And she had no idea why her mind was showing her a barn when they were obviously investigating an arson at an industrial site.

"Good," Williams said. "Who did it?"

Sacco shrank in his seat in embarrassment.

"Two men," Nancy replied. "One is about five-ten , maybe one eighty, one ninety. He has dark hair and drags one leg slightly. He is clean shaven, maybe early thirties, round face. The other is blond, a lot younger. Maybe nineteen, twenty. He is strong; he may lift weights. He's fit-looking, trim. Green eyes. It's odd, you would think they would be nervous doing something like this, but they don't seem at all worried."

"But," she finished, "they didn't burn down a building. They burned down a barn." She braced for Williams's comment but none came. When she looked up, the two men were staring at her. Williams looked dumbstruck. Sacco was surprised, but a grin was spreading slowly across his lips.

"We better move," Williams finally said, "before somebody calls the cops and we have to explain this to them."

They pulled out of the parking lot and drove until Williams found a sandy pull-off along the road. Meanwhile, Sacco was pawing through the file, which now sat on his lap.

"I smelled kerosene," Nancy continued. "And there was a tarpaulin on the floor. They used candles somehow. I saw them placing them on the tarpaulin. And there is another smell too, gasoline. But mainly it's the kerosene."

Sacco pulled out the original investigator's notes and scanned them.

With Williams momentarily silenced, Nancy returned to the scene—*only now fire raged through the barn, melting and twisting steel. Although she had little experience with fires, the intensity with which the flames consumed the building and its contents surprised her.*

"It was a very hot fire," she said.

"That's a kerosene fire. Gasoline explodes, but kerosene burns hot," Williams explained.

Nancy wondered why she was getting a barn when they were clearly investigating a commercial arson. But she knew too well that factual information could skew her reading, so she determined to save her questions and keep rolling.

"Why?" Sacco asked. "Why would he destroy all his equipment just to collect insurance on it?"

"He didn't destroy it all," she said.

Both men wheeled on her.

"He took out three pieces of equipment."

Sacco pulled out the insurance list as Nancy continued.

"One piece is an International Harvester combine, another is a tractor of some kind—a John Deere, I think. I know it is."

"There *is* a Harvester combine on the list." Sacco's finger raced down the page. "And a Deere combine too."

"No, I saw the Deere combine destroyed," Nancy said.

"Let me see that," Williams said. He grabbed the list from Sacco's hands. "Get the photos of the scene out."

Nancy was now hunched forward, peering between the split back of the car's bench seats. Williams put the insurance list down and retrieved the fire marshal's photos of the scene. After a minute he looked up at Sacco. "It's three short. Didn't anybody count the hulks?"

Sacco shrugged.

Williams shook his head. "Okay, Nancy," he said. "Now how do we prove it?" His tone wasn't entirely sarcastic.

Nancy sat back and asked herself the question. *The image that came into her mind was an older man with loose, porous skin hanging from prominent jowls. His nose was bulbous and red and he wore thick glasses. She pulled back and saw he was in a blue uniform. And with the image came an awareness that this man knew what had happened that night.*

She described the image to Williams and Sacco, but neither knew quite what to make of it.

"Oh, and this might help," she continued. "He's stored the equipment on other property he owns."

Williams looked at Sacco. Could the man they were looking for have been that stupid? It would be easy enough to check.

An hour later Williams pulled into an old gas station near Bear, Delaware, called Tony's Gulf. It consisted of two pumps and a small shack that served as an office. A red, round-shouldered Coke machine sat next to the open door.

On the drive up from Dover, Sacco had started to share with her details of the White case, but she stopped him, asking only for the date and the victim's name. When they arrived, Williams and Sacco walked inside and she could hear Williams making small talk with somebody.

She hung back, unsure of what to do. For a brief moment, she wandered outside the office without direction, her mind focusing on the name Jack White. Suddenly her legs refused to move. Her body was frozen, rooted where she stood. She looked up to scream and stared into the harsh glare of an overhanging streetlight. What had been a brilliant afternoon was now ink-black night, and the night was held back only by the circle of artificial light that shown down on Tony's Gulf. Screams and a young boy's pleading for mercy drew her inside the office, where metal smacked against human flesh. A searing pain grabbed her spine like a steel hand and exploded out her back. The wounded muscles coiled like a nest of frightened snakes, cutting her in half. A thousand images rushed past in a great blur, pulling the air out of her lungs. She was sick, trying to wretch.

"Are you having trouble?" The voice was familiar, steadying, nearby.

Nancy blinked and it was afternoon again. Sacco was looking at her with concern.

Disoriented, Nancy shook her head.

"I don't know. I can't seem to move."

Williams was watching from a few feet away, his arms folded over his chest. He and Sacco exchanged looks.

"Go ahead and tell her, Carl," Sacco said.

Instead Williams walked to the car. Clearly he was wrestling with something.

"I can't do much from here. I need to get a little distance," Nancy murmured. Sacco steadied her and they walked to the car, where she leaned up against the door.

"Tell me what?" she asked.

"That spot where you were standing. That's where they found him."

Nancy was not surprised, but it upset her deeply. A nightmare was one thing, but to know that she had just reexperienced what a human being had actually gone through was almost intolerable. The hate and anger pounding away at his helpless body had filled her with horror. Sacco's voice swam away from her as the vision started to return. She became dizzy and took a deep breath.

"Are you all right?" Sacco asked.

Nancy nodded. She stood another minute, gathering her strength. Then she started.

"I get three men. These men had come in to rob him, but he challenged them. Jack was not the kind of person to just let that happen. He couldn't do that. He had to defend the station, which was foolish, but he was a little macho. There was something about the way he interacted with the men that prompted the attack. There are three of them, two off to the side, watching. The one who hurt him is a big man, probably a weight lifter, certainly strong and angry. He goes out-of-control brutal. He just flipped out. Once he started beating Jack, he couldn't stop. It was so easy."

"Can you tell me what he looks like?" Sacco pulled out a notebook.

Nancy closed her eyes briefly, then blinked them open. She was rerunning the episode, but carefully and from a distance.

"Muscular, very homely face, and his nose looks like a boxer's nose, kind of mashed."

"Race?"

"White, all are white," she said. "He has a long criminal record—burglary, armed robbery—and he is vicious."

Williams sat in the front seat of the car. Occasionally pieces of the conversation would drift in to him. None of it impressed him very much, which he found comforting. It helped him deal with what she had said at the arson site.

"Do you have a map?" Nancy asked.

Sacco asked Williams if there was a map in the car.

"Delaware," he said.

"A state map do?" Sacco asked Nancy.

"Not enough detail."

"Why do you need a map?" Williams asked.

"So I can show you where he lives."

"You can do that?" Even Sacco was incredulous.

"I don't know. It worked with the houseboat."

The troop was a quaint, red brick building on Route 13 near the Wilmington Airport, only a few miles from Tony's Gulf. Williams decided it was their best bet for a detailed map.

He pulled into the commander's spot close to the door and was the first out of the car. By the time Sacco opened Nancy's door, Williams had disappeared into the building. "Got to make a call," was all he said.

There was nothing quaint about the inside. The building's defining quality was security. If it had an architectural theme,

Nancy decided it was cold discomfort. The only piece of furniture was a wooden bench with a narrow seat and torturous posts for a back. Sacco seated Nancy there while he made arrangements for her to go upstairs. Sacco said they needed an interrogation room and a detailed map of Wilmington.

They did not see Williams again until they were in the room with a map spread out on the table.

Nancy stood over it, her head cocked to one side, looking toward the wall. Actual names distracted and confused her. She centered the large muscular man in her consciousness and allowed her hand to run gently over the smooth folds of the map. The paper was cool to the touch, not the least bit distinctive, not until she felt a warmth under her palm. She moved a finger toward the spot.

"He lives here," she said.

Sacco crowded closer to see where she was pointing. The first name he noticed was St. Francis Hospital. He took out a note pad and jotted down some intersecting streets.

Next stop was the Alfred I. Du Pont Institute, a world-renowned orthopaedic hospital north of Wilmington. Jack White's room was small and to Nancy surprisingly empty of the equipment usually found in hospital rooms. Other than the bed and a straight-backed chair, there was only a bedside table with a small portable radio playing softly.

When they first entered, Sacco moved toward the bed to see if there had been any change since his last visit. Williams stayed in the hall.

As emotionally wrenching as the day had been, nothing that had come before had prepared Nancy for the sight of Jack White. He was a small boy to begin with—only five-four and thin. He had once weighed 130 pounds. Comatose and unable to eat, he had been losing weight ever since the beating in February. His arms were curled protectively, legs tucked up to his chest in a fetal posture, hands clamped tightly shut in a perpetual spasm causing him to vibrate slightly. His mouth was open, as if poised for a scream that he could not utter.

Nancy was used to a certain level of activity in human minds. There was activity in Jack, but it was at a frighteningly low level. What she felt was terror. In Jack's world, the beating was still going on. Was he trapped in a moment like her own nightmare at the gas station? The thought sent a shiver through her.

Jack was lying on his side, facing away from the door. His eyes were closed and except for the tremor, he seemed not to be there. Nancy stood behind him, trying to adjust. She instinctively reached out with her mind to comfort him. A cry of anguish lashed out at her open psyche. Jack was very much there.

She moved around to face him, closed her eyes, then kept saying mentally, *Calm down, you are safe now. You are in the hospital.*

A startled gasp from Sacco brought her back into the room. Jack's eyes, which had been open, were now staring up at her.

"Do you think that's a reflex?" Sacco asked. He crossed to the other side of the bed, behind Jack.

"I don't know," Nancy said, but she did not think so. The tremor had subsided and he seemed calmer.

A black attendant pushed into the room to shift Jack's position, and Nancy sensed a flash of fear from Jack. The attendant was a young man, strong, and protective of his patients. He had a gentle manner and took great pains to ensure that he turned the injured boy as gently as possible. Nancy wondered why Jack had reacted to him with fear. Or was it her imagination?

The attendant was used to an audience, but normally it was family.

"He can't really understand what's going on," he volunteered.

Out of Jack came a low guttural sound, primitive and almost inaudible.

"Awwggggggggggg."

"That's not right," Nancy said quickly. The words popped out. "He can understand what's going on. He can't say anything, but he can understand you."

Jack seemed to relax. He was still looking at Nancy.

"No, no, no, there's too much damage. He can't—" the

attendant began.

"Awwgggggggggggggggg."

"He's answering you," Nancy said. "He's telling you in his limited way that you are wrong. He can hear you and he can understand you."

"He just does that every now and then," the attendant continued.

"Maybe you should pay attention to when Jack does that," Nancy insisted, "because he is trying to talk to you."

The attendant smiled at her, seemingly willing to let it drop if he could just get on with his work. He turned Jack over, facing him away from Nancy and the sound returned, only this time it did not stop.

Sacco looked instinctively toward the door for a doctor and saw Williams pacing.

"I think he wants you. I think that's why he's doing it," Sacco said. Nancy came around to the side of the bed where Sacco now stood and saw Jack looking up at him with what she felt was anger. When Nancy walked into his line of vision, the sound subsided.

There was thinking going on in there, she was sure of it. He was trapped, but he was not without thought.

She slipped her hand around his knotted left fist and felt his body relax even more. Through his hand she felt the faint tremor that, though lessened, still vibrated his frame. His skin was dry, but she noticed that his forehead was perspiring from the exertion. She withdrew her hand, intending to rinse out a rag and wipe his brow. But when she pulled her hand away, the groan returned.

"Awwgggggggggggggggg."

Just a minute, she said. *I'm going to rinse this wash rag out and I'm going to get the perspiration off your forehead and you're going to calm down.*

"Awwgggggggggggggggg."

Calm down, Jack, I can hear you. You don't have to yell for me. I can hear you in my mind.

Nancy believed she saw flickers of recognition in his eyes. She tried to explain to him who she was and what they were trying to do, but whenever she thought of the assault, his body tightened visibly, he vibrated and growled. She quickly gave up.

Forget about it. Put it out of your mind and concentrate on getting well. Try every way you can to make people understand that you are here and that you can understand.

She stroked his forehead. From the radio came a familiar refrain by the Silver Convention: "Fly, robin, fly / Up, up to the sky…"

Mom's song, she heard in her mind. It startled her. She looked into Jack's eyes, but he wasn't there, yet the thought was so clear. *Mom's song.*

And Jack's racked and exhausted body seemed finally to rest.

Williams was sitting in a chair along the corridor wall when he saw Sacco and Nancy walking toward him. Neither said anything, and it surprised him that Sacco was not peppering Nancy with questions. He rose as they passed and they all three walked wordlessly out of the building.

It was Nancy who finally broke the silence.

"That wasn't much help," she reflected as Williams pulled the car out of the hospital lot.

"I think he knew we were there, though," Sacco said. "I'll tell the family that he seemed to respond to you."

"If you are talking to them, ask them about that song, 'Fly, Robin, Fly,'" Nancy said.

"What about it?"

"When it came on the radio, I thought I heard Jack say, 'Mom's song.' In fact, I'm sure I did."

Little else was said. They arrived at Nancy's house about twenty minutes later, and even Williams seemed sincere when he thanked Nancy for her efforts. He wasn't sure they would amount to much, but, well, he wanted to thank her anyway.

Inside, the drapes were drawn, softening the rays from the late sun that pushed through the fabric. She didn't bother opening them. The muffled light made her feel private and safe. George met her with his usual barrage of barking and bounded up on her knees for a head rub. She gave him a token pat and fell back onto the sofa. George curled up beside her.

She was drained, but the day had resolved something for her: No matter how much polite police harassment Colonel Smith dished out, she would not do police work.

I am too sensitive. It's just too much. This isn't going to be good for me.

Another thought struck. *What if I'm wrong? That will be better because then he won't even ask me to work any more cases.*

But secretly she knew she didn't want to be wrong. She wanted to be right. She wanted to help find the man who had taken Jack White's life away from him. The man who had beaten him senseless and left him to spend the rest of his days in a crippled and maimed body with half a mind. If she could help get that man, well, that would be worth this day—this day that had seemed like twenty.

She had no idea how long she sat on the sofa, but eventually the door opened and Blake and Travis came piling through, trailed by their father. The invasion snapped her back. In an instant the quiet room was awash in sunlight and chatter and George's relentless barking.

Blake, as always, led the charge, making sure he was center stage with Mom. They had been shopping, but even while wandering through the mall, he had held on to the picture that he now pushed in her face. Nancy took the sheet of construction paper in self-defense and held it back far enough to see. Blobs of color and stick figures covered most of the page. A sun was setting behind a little house.

"Go put this on the refrigerator where your grandmother will be sure to see it," Nancy told him.

Blake smiled from ear to ear. He knew their grandmother was an artist, and if Mom wanted Guppy to see it, it must be good. He headed for the kitchen.

"I don't have any picture, Mom," said Travis.

"That's okay, T-bird, I don't think there's any more room on the refrigerator anyway. How about a hug? That's about as good as a picture anyway."

The little boy beamed and wrapped his arms around her neck, planting a big kiss on her forehead. "What's for dinner?" he asked.

Nancy suddenly realized she hadn't given it a thought. Nor had she eaten since breakfast. She looked helplessly up at John. "Ponderosa?"

"Oh, boy," said Travis. "Can we, Dad?"

John didn't have much choice. "Get washed up," he said.

As Travis bounded happily away toward the bathroom, she thought again of Jack White, twisted and staring from his hospital bed. For some reason the lyrics to the song came into her head: "Fly, robin, fly / Up, up to the sky…"; *Mom's song.*

Maybe, she thought, *if Colonel Smith calls, and if anything I did today pans out, maybe I should help after all.*

Three

The Opening

*T*he restaurant's noisy chatter, the hissing and aroma of grilling steaks, and the children's happy faces failed to do their usual job of lifting Nancy's spirits. She was tired and anxious. She felt on the edge of a change in her life and she did not grasp what it would mean. Where was this ability taking her? Was working with the police her life's work? She had always felt that she would end up doing important work, but she thought functioning as a psychic would be more spiritual than practical. Certainly that's the message she had gotten as a child.

Thinking of her childhood made her miss her father. Somehow Fred Myer had always been associated in her mind with her special gifts. But now her father was gone. He had died suddenly five years before while visiting his sister in Newport News, Virginia. It was late at night when the chest pains had struck and his brother-in-law, John Massey, a well-respected local cardiologist, knew exactly what to do. He did not wait for an ambulance but drove Fred at speeds topping ninety miles an hour from Newport News to Richmond, Virginia, a full eighty miles to what he considered the best cardiac care unit on the East Coast. But even the staff there could not save him; the damage was too great. Sometime during the night on Halloween, 1971, Fred Myer's heart had quit.

Nancy and her father were especially close. While Fred had the knack of making each of his children feel this special bond, Nancy had observed things about him that made her feel he shared her special gifts.

He would not have called these gifts psychic, but then, when she first experienced them as a child, that is not how she saw them either. They were just useful things that people could do when they needed to, as natural as the way you saw a face when you thought of a name or the way your legs took you someplace you wanted to go.

But as she grew older, she found that she and her father could do things other people could not. There was, for instance, the way she and her father could talk to animals. She knew that's what she could do, and though she never asked him directly about it, she assumed it was what he was doing when time after time he managed to calm frightened and violent creatures in the many villages where they were posted. In Chile, the villagers used to refer to him as "*mágico*."

Then too, his wisdom seemed to exceed logic, but Nancy would never know for sure if this was a child's natural perception of a bright and sensitive parent or true prescience. God, she wished she could sit down with him now and go over what was happening to her.

She searched her mind for how it had all begun and found herself transported from the noisy restaurant to a dusty, sunbaked street in the small village of Chillán, Chile.

Nancy, then nine, had accompanied the maids to the marketplace, as she often did, and as was typical, she found native Gypsies coming up to her, jabbering away in their native language. Although it was not Spanish, which she had quickly learned, or English, she somehow found that if she focused on their thoughts, she could grasp their meaning. What she found at first terrified her. They wanted Nancy as their own.

According to the maids, it was not uncommon for the Gypsies to steal children, but it was unusually bold for them to approach the daughter of an American state department employee. The maids were clearly frightened of them and warned Nancy not even to look at them or speak with them. They had powerful magic and could control you with their eyes, they said. She tried to obey, although it was impossible to completely ignore the strangers.

Nancy found that as the months passed during their posting in Chillán, the Gypsies became bolder and bolder, giving Nancy small trinkets and laughing as the maids timidly tried to shoo them away.

Nancy, like any nine-year-old, had grown numb to the danger and had actually found herself drawn to these happy, free-spirited people. In some odd way she began to feel a kinship with them, and as she did, her guard slipped.

On this day a large number of Gypsies were gathered under the shade of an awning, surrounding a handsome old man whom Nancy had never seen before. She was startled to find his words drifting into her mind.

"Come to me, child," he said. Nancy felt no fear, only love and warmth as she drew toward the crowd despite the protest of the maids.

"Police, police!" screamed one of the older domestics, fearing Nancy was about to be abducted.

A carabinero who happened to be a friend of Nancy's father came running across the square to investigate the trouble. The maid pointed to the old Gypsy.

"I only wish to meet this special child," the Gypsy leader told the carabinero in Spanish.

The officer hauled himself up to his full height and answered in his most authoritative manner. "Meet her, but know that she is an American. If you steal her, they will send armies to protect her."

The Gypsy looked Nancy straight in the eyes and laughed. "Even you and all your armies could not steal this one unless she wanted to be stolen," he said. The men around him laughed.

Smiling at Nancy, he again called in his mind.

No, she answered firmly in her own mind. *I don't want to go with you. That is not what I am to do and you know it.*

The old man nodded. To the entire gathering he said, "This child has stars around her head. She can foretell the future and heal. She will be a great teacher. God must have important work for one to whom he has given so much. Never before have I seen one with so many gifts. I have heard of children like this born to other tribes, but I have never seen one before."

Then he laughed wickedly. "In the old days, before I was wise, I would have stolen her. But not this one, not now. Angered, she would bring great woe to my people."

Nancy smiled at his insight into her temperament. She thought it strange that she felt so relaxed, so comfortable with this man. She wondered what he meant by stars.

No sooner had the question framed itself in her mind than she saw in his eyes a flash, and then she was looking through them—through his eyes—at a child much like herself, only this girl was surrounded by a shimmering energy band that seemed to snap and pop with large flashes. With a start she realized it was herself she was seeing. Around her head the flashes looked like the stars in the ink-black Chilean night. They were lovely but somehow frightening. There was something about what they portended about her future that stirred anxiety deep within her. In the hot noon sun of Chillán she felt a shiver of ice run through her. Visions of dead bodies appeared to her.

Suddenly she was again looking at the old man. He rose and reached out. A surge of energy moved through her as his finger brushed her cheek.

Don't let your destiny scare you, child, he said. *God is watching out for you.*

You're like me! she thought with wonderment and relief.

The flash in his eyes dimmed and he seemed for that moment just a lonely old man. *Finding another eases the loneliness.*

Does it get worse? she asked.

It is bearable, he said. He started to reach out to touch her again but pulled his hand back as the carabinero stepped protectively between them.

The incident was never far from Nancy's consciousness from that moment forward. It brought her both comfort and sadness, but at least it helped her better understand some of the things she did that no one else seemed able to do.

One was her ability to see into the past. For instance, she might be at a ruin and wonder what it had been like in its heyday. Suddenly she would find herself observing a scene from that time and place.

Once in Lima, Peru, she stood staring in fascination at the centuries-old remains of an Incan child that had been found high in the Andes. Preserved by the ice, the mummified remains were intact, clothing and all. As she looked at this tiny, shriveled body, she was startled to see a healthy set of sparkling eyes staring back at her. With a shocking suddenness she could see him playing in a temple. She could see that his short life had been a privileged one, with servants to care for his every need. From the deference he was paid, Nancy could see that he seemed to be worshiped, but this had brought with it isolation. He had everything but friendship; loneliness plagued him. In a subsequent image he was ill, alternately burning with fever and shaking with chills. Nancy pulled back instinctively to gain some distance and watched as his parents, a shaman, and servants worked to save him. Next she saw row upon row of people mourning his passing. The vision dissolved in her own sad tears.

Fascinated with this new mental toy, she used it frequently as she and her family toured the ruins of old Inca towns. Although she was too young to think of ferreting out evidential details, she had not a shred of doubt that what she was seeing was absolutely real. It did not occur to her that it could be anything else.

Visions of the present day were different. They were clearer and the colors were more vibrant. They seemed more like real life to her. They could be warnings or lessons in handling her abilities. But like the scenes from the past, they often were like movies running freely and frequently through her thoughts. Sometimes they came in response to concerns she carried with her.

Waiting to ship out to their first overseas posting, Nancy was both terrified and fascinated by what awaited her. She was only five, but information about the coming changes came to her in recurring dreams and visions. Though she was too young to understand all of what was being shown to her, it no doubt helped prepare her for the strangeness and hardships that awaited her in Brazil's Amazon jungle. One vivid vision later occurred exactly as it had appeared to her. She saw her mother leading her and her sister Susan to bed. Her mother stopped the girls at the doorway of their room and turned on the lights. Large, frightening black bugs scurried in all directions, clacking across the wooden floors.

She frequently had visions of butterflies, clouds of them. They were colored a lustrous turquoise she had never seen before. She liked to sit still and call them to land all over her. Later, after they had arrived in Brazil, she realized that this vision too had been more than imagination. The turquoise butterflies were every- where, and she found that whenever fear threatened her, she would think of how fragile they were and yet how well they survived in this hostile land. If they could survive, perhaps she could as well. She would call them and they would come.

Sometimes Nancy would sit bolt upright in bed from visions of large snakes hanging from trees and slithering through branches, becoming visible and invisible as their protective coloring matched and contrasted with the ferns, vines, and shadows of the jungle in which they lived.

The vision that touched her most deeply was the stark beauty and danger of a sleek black panther, the lean muscles of its shiny body rippling as it prowled through the ferns for food. In her vision, its silent progress was marked only by the screech of fleeing monkeys and birds. She stared deeply into its golden eyes, mesmerized, and it gazed back, penetrating her very soul. They seemed to understand each other. Nancy soon found that from this dream she developed a kinship with all large cats. When she visited zoos, the cats, be they lions or tigers—or panthers—would wake up and gaze into her eyes. They studied her every move. It was five years later, during their second posting to Chillán, that she had the opportunity to test her rapport with large cats. When the opportunity came, her very life rested in the balance.

As an agricultural specialist, Nancy's father pursued almost limitless duties. They ranged from teaching the native Chileans modern farming and canning techniques to helping them repair and rebuild farm equipment. In between, he taught basic veterinary techniques, first aid, nutrition—whatever was needed. In the Chilean fall of 1956, what was needed north of Chillán near the mountains was a good hunter. A man-eating puma was attacking the villages and had seriously injured several of the villagers. Everyone knew that once a lion had begun attacking humans, it would return again and again until it was killed.

Fred Myer learned of this animal while on a visit with Nancy to a farm in the area and was immediately recruited because he was known as a crack shot. He could not decline, despite his concerns about taking Nancy on a puma hunt. Still, he reasoned it would be safer for her to be with the armed party than left behind as easy prey in the village. As they awaited the others, Nancy listened to the talk of this monster that was terrifying the villages. As the story of the attacks was retold, the ferocity of the animal responsible seemed to grow, along with the damage to the men who now lay in the hospital maimed by it. Nancy couldn't help trying to imagine the attack, but when she did, the vision she got was much different from what she had heard described.

She was transported to a clearing deep in the forest. Before her stood the man-eater. To Nancy he seemed anything but fierce as he looked pleadingly into her eyes and she experienced the pain that emanated from his right front foot. Directing her attention downward, she saw instantly that two of his toes were missing and the stumps that remained were gnarled and bloody. They seemed badly infected. She reached out and energy passed from her hand to the wounded paw as she petted the animal's huge head.

The enthusiasm of the conversation around her broke through her reverie.

"It's hurt," she said. "Its paw is hurt and it can't hunt. That's why it's attacking the village. Couldn't you just feed it until its paw heals?"

She was mortified when she realized what she had said and whom she had said it to. She looked to her father for help, but before he could respond, one of the villagers had jumped to his feet and moved quickly toward Nancy.

"How did you know this?" he asked. Then he turned to the others. "The trackers say it has two toes missing on its right front foot. How did you know this?"

This time Nancy knew better than to speak.

"She probably heard the children talking about it." She heaved a sigh of relief as her father came to her rescue. He cast her a warning glare to keep still.

Fred was a respected man and his explanation was accepted immediately, if only temporarily.

The hunt began. After several hours Nancy found the strict rule her father had set about staying close behind him didn't seem as urgent as it had in the excitement of the morning. She started to stray off the path and into the forest, or down the path and ahead of the group. As long as she could sense the group and hear them behind her, she felt safe. So it was with a sense of security that she darted playfully out and around a bend in the trail and came face to face with the man-eater.

The scene was exactly as she had envisioned. The lion looked deeply into her eyes and stretched its head forward to touch her hand. Nancy reached out to it. She was oddly without fear. A surge of energy passed between them. *Flee to the mountains*, she urged. *Do not attack the villages. Men are coming to kill you because you attacked their villages.* Love from the animal washed over her as the sound of her father's voice, at once commanding and frightened, ripped through the air behind her. *"Run!,"* Nancy screamed both out loud and in her mind.

"Down," her father's voice commanded almost in the same instant. "Get down so we can get a shot. Drop down."

But she did not. Instead she stood and watched in wonder as the wounded lion gently sniffed her again, then slipped into the forest away from the hunting party. The villagers rushed around her protectively and Fred's arms engulfed her as he dropped his gun and fell to one knee, wrapping her in a bear hug.

"It's okay, Dad," Nancy said when he finally pushed her out to arm's length and checked her for injuries. "He won't be back. He's going to the mountains to heal."

Shaking from the residue of adrenaline that had pumped wildly through his veins, he could only hug and hold his daughter as they heard futile shots fired after the fleeing lion.

"He was just hurt and hungry, Dad."

But Fred could not yet speak. In their embrace neither noticed the hunters returning, nor did they immediately see the tracker cautiously studying Nancy and gazing at her with awe.

"Esta niña es una bruja," he said to the others. He bowed slightly to Nancy and gently touched her sleeve.

"What does he mean, Dad?"

"That's what they call their medicine men. He's honoring you. Thank him."

He rose and turned, thanking the man for honoring his daughter with such a title.

"Thank you," Nancy said, not quite understanding his deference.

The attacks stopped and the three-toed lion was not seen again in the Chillán area in all the time Nancy and her family were posted there.

The memories of her father brought tears to her eyes. Travis was the first to notice.

"Hey, Mom, don't you like your steak?" he asked.

"It's fine." Nancy laughed, pulled back into the restaurant and looking incongruous with tears on her cheeks and a smile turning up the corners of her mouth. "I was just thinking of something sad."

"Grandpa Fred," said Blake without interrupting his attack on his own meal.

She marveled at how kids had a way of keeping you rooted in the here and now. Maybe she had done that for her father; she wished she could have done so much more.

Even into her adulthood their bond was deep and close. In the twenty-six years Nancy had lived before her father's death, she had failed to find another human being who could match his wisdom, compassion, and character. His death left her with an aching emptiness that time seemed unable to fill.

Watching her boys devouring their steaks, she was once again pulled back to the roots of her psychic opening. She allowed herself to go, still searching for some guidance on how best to use her gifts. She thought back to when the doors to her psychic gifts flew open in a frighteningly dramatic way. It had started in the spring of 1973 with a friend's game.

Despite her world travels, Nancy had never seen a Ouija board before. At first its decorative design and mysterious floating pointer were irresistible fun. She was introduced to it by her friend Mary Ann Bogar, who brought it over for fun one afternoon while the children were napping. Nancy was quite surprised to feel their fingers pulled over the board by what seemed like a lifelike willfulness as the pointer spelled out answers to their questions. At first she thought Mary Ann was pushing the pointer, but her friend admonished her, "Just touch it lightly. Don't push it around the board." "I thought *you* were pushing it," Nancy said.

The two women looked at each other and laughed.

They had so much fun that it became almost a daily ritual. Then one day Nancy asked if she could keep the board to show John. That evening, she pulled it out from its closet hiding place after the kids had been put to bed and explained to John how it worked.

The two put their fingers on the pointer, just as she and Mary Ann had, but this time nothing happened. It was lifeless. When Nancy called Mary Ann the next day to ask what might account for such an odd thing, Mary Ann said only that it doesn't work for some people, but she had no idea why.

So when Mary Ann and her husband Bill came by a few nights later, the two women demonstrated the Ouija while the men watched.

"Is Bill going to make more money at his job or get another job?" "Will we be successful in adopting a child?"

"Will it be a boy or girl?"

"What color will its hair be?"

But then the Ouija started moving on its own. Without the benefit of a question, it spelled out the name of a dead relative of the Bogars for which it claimed to speak. Although fascinating, the eerie way in which it seemed to exhibit certain personality traits of the deceased frightened Mary Ann and they soon abandoned the game.

But Nancy was beginning to wonder if it was just a game. The next day after putting the kids down for their nap, she found herself unable to get the Ouija out of her mind, even though she had no idea how she could play without another person. She reached up into the closet where they had hidden it from Blake's inquiring eyes, pulled it down, and read the instructions. It didn't say you shouldn't use it by yourself, only that it probably wouldn't work.

But it did. Very well. The pointer flew with greater speed and purpose than even when she had worked it with Mary Ann. Working it alone removed any doubt from Nancy's mind that the movement of the pointer was controlled by the player. It was frightening, exhilarating, and irresistible.

At first she tried to think of questions the answers to which could not come from her own subsconscious. She thought perhaps that she should ask about world politics. Or if she asked about a local election in which she had no interest, after the election she could validate the Ouija's accuracy. But before she could pose these questions, the Ouija started talking to her.

The message was one she had heard before, but not since childhood. The speaker, identifying itself as Anna Dearworth, said that Nancy had special gifts and an important job to do and that she should get started on it. It said she was wasting her life. It also warned her to stop playing with the Ouija.

Nancy had never been completely happy in the role of house-wife, though she dearly loved her children. What the board was telling her was flattering, so flattering that she decided the message was just coming from some part of herself that represented the discontented side of her personality. She put the board away.

But the next day at the boy's nap time she once again found herself talking to Anna Dearworth through the Ouija. This time Anna tried to convince Nancy that she was an ancestor. And she continued to drive home the message that Nancy had a mission, that she was unique and would have to face up to it. The next time Nancy talked to her mother, she asked about the name Anna Dearworth, but her mother knew of no such person in the family.

Nancy's sessions with Anna continued for about three days before Anna told Nancy that she was having trouble maintaining the connection and might not be able to continue to communicate with her. Sure enough, on the fourth day the information spelled out by the Ouija became garbled and childish. It said, "Your mother is coming," but her mother never arrived. It was one of its favorite predictions.

Still, Nancy couldn't quit playing with it. The pointer moved so easily that its fluid motion seemed to hypnotize her. The change in his wife began to worry John, who tried to get her to quit using it. One method he used was to demonstrate that it was lying to them. This was not hard, but even knowledge that the information coming from the Ouija was garbage and largely useless did not break its growing hold on Nancy.

One time when the board had again predicted that Nancy's mother, Harriet, was coming from Dover, they immediately called her. There was no answer. They waited, but she did not show up. When they called back several hours later, Harriet answered the phone and told them she had never intended to come to their house but had only gone shopping.

"See?" John said to the Ouija. "Your information is wrong. You are a liar. We have checked your information and it is wrong. How do you explain that?"

It was the most direct challenge they had yet made to the Ouija and its response was just as direct. It chilled them both.

"F-U-C-K-Y-O-U," it said.

Nancy, shocked, pulled her hands off the pointer.

It continued to move on its own.

"B-I-T-C-H," the board said.

But even that episode was not enough to break its hold on Nancy. She continued to haul it out whenever she could find the time.

Though the quality of information coming from the board itself was deteriorating, Nancy's direct psychic activity seemed to be growing in volume, detail, and clarity. Although she had always used her psychic ability to keep track of Blake, she was now so tuned in to his mischief that he actually noticed and complained about it.

One day while washing dishes at the kitchen sink, she suddenly without warning had a picture of Blake and her neighbor Marty's little girl, Mary, playing with lawn chemicals in Marty's shed. Nancy knew she didn't have time to get there herself, so she called her neighbor. Marty ran to the garage and found the two exactly as Nancy had described.

On another occasion, Travis came to her clearly upset, but as usual it was almost impossible to get him to talk about what was bothering him. This time Nancy somehow knew that Blake had broken one of his toys and hidden it.

"Did Blake break your toy?" she said to him.

Travis burst into tears. It turned out that it was one of his favorites, a Fisher-Price rescue truck with a cherry picker extension on it. It was a very sturdy toy that would have required considerable effort to break.

Nancy walked right to where Blake had hidden the pieces and announced that he would now give Travis *his* rescue truck. Blake was too stunned by his mother's sudden omniscience to argue.

Another day during this period Nancy had a sense that something awful was about to happen to Blake. She shot out the door just as the trash man came hauling the boy up to her by his collar. Blake had been playing in the back of their trash truck and nearly found himself compacted. Only his screams and the alert driver had saved him.

Along with playing in trash trucks, Blake liked to sneak into the yard of a state trooper who lived near the Andersons and get back out without being eaten by the trooper's attack dog, Cogill. While her picking up on this favorite sortie had formerly been hit or miss, Nancy now found that every time Blake was getting ready to cross the street heading for Cogill's yard, a part of her would say, *Blake is going after Cogill.*

The change in the volume of her psychic activity was not limited to information about the children. Before she had started playing with the Ouija, messages would sometimes come in a whisper, faint and indistinct. Many times the voice was so quiet that she would miss it or block it out. Now the messages were much too loud to be missed.

She had always had a good intuitive sense of whether people were okay or in trouble, but she didn't necessarily know what was going on in their heads. Similarly, she could tell if someone was in a really bad mood. Now if she wanted to know why they were in a bad mood she would only have to ask herself and a voice would answer.

Worse, the information now often came unbidden. She could be standing in line at the supermarket, for instance, and bits of the internal dialogues people around her were carrying on in their own minds would begin to swim into her consciousness. Phrases and feelings that were not hers intruded into her thoughts.

There was also a major battle going on between the source of the Ouija's information and the information she was getting directly. Her own voice was telling her that the Ouija was dangerous and unreliable. Yet it had only been since she started fooling with the Ouija that this voice had become so loud and distinct. Her inner voice was like going to church; the Ouija was more like a house of horrors in an amusement park. Both had their appeal, though the Ouija was becoming more and more problematic as the weeks went by.

John continued his campaign to get rid of it, somehow grasping instinctively that if he were to take matters into his own hands, its hold on Nancy would not be broken. She had to do it, but she seemed unable. It wasn't until the poltergeist activity began that Nancy resolved to get the Ouija out of their lives.

They were sitting at their kitchen table one evening that summer after putting the children to bed. The Ouija board sat between them in its closed box and John was declaring his intent to break its hold on Nancy. He then got up to pour them both a glass of grape juice. The whole family adored Welch's grape juice, so Nancy always bought the biggest jug she could find. After filling their glasses, John sat it back on the counter and only partially screwed the lid back on.

He returned to the table and his argument. "Or we could just take it outside and rip it to shreds and put it in the garbage," he said.

No sooner were the words out of his mouth than the bottle of grape juice lifted straight off the counter, wheeled toward John, and smashed directly onto the floor in front of him. A fountain of grape juice flew up to the ceiling and sprayed the entire kitchen.

The next morning Nancy was up early. She marched into the kitchen, resolved to take the Ouija into the backyard and destroy it. But no sooner had she entered the kitchen than the game flew across the table and smashed into the wall. It fell to the floor and just sat there, challenging.

Nancy was so frightened she busied herself with household

chores, hiding her anxiety from the children. She kept clear of the fallen Ouija, though her eyes were constantly drawn to it. Finally, it was nap time. She put the children down, carefully closing the doors to their rooms as she walked back into the kitchen and stared at the game box on the floor. Even in her fear, she felt drawn to operate it.

From somewhere deep within her came a commanding *No.*

She somehow felt bolstered by it. It was a voice she could trust, one that had guided her through many crises in her life and invariably had given her good advice.

She knew what she had to do and that it had to be done at that moment. She wanted her life back. She wanted out from under the influence of this thing that had lied to her and sworn at her. As she recalled these things, the rage welled up in her and strengthened her resolve. She would do battle with whatever was necessary to rid herself of this thing; once that thought had formed, she felt assurance flow through her. The resources to defeat it would be made available to her.

She marched into the children's bedroom and woke them, then shepherded them over to their neighbor's to finish their naps. She returned to the kitchen and grabbed the game box from the floor and a hammer from the junk drawer. With the board grasped tightly in her hand, she strode into the backyard and with little ceremony let loose the rage she felt. She smashed the hammer into the box's ornate face. The Ouija itself she demolished with a few quick strokes, then stuffed it all in a garbage can and returned to the house. She sat at her kitchen table, relishing her bold act. She felt very good—safe for the first time in many weeks.

The poltergeist activity never returned, but the psychic functioning that the Ouija had opened up never left. Nancy now set about managing the flood of information that streamed into her consciousness. It was not always a burden. Just as she found it handy to be able to track Blake more effectively, Nancy now found that many times all she would have to do to find a solution to a problem was to ask.

"What you thinking up, Mom?"

Suddenly she was back in the Ponderosa Steak House.

"Mom," Blake repeated.

"What to tell Colonel Smith," Nancy said.

"There's a question?" John asked.

"It was harder than I thought today," she said. "There was a young man in a coma from a beating and it was pretty awful. Even the detectives who took me to the hospital to see him had a hard time with it. I don't think I did much to help. Not on the case, anyhow. But you know, I think I touched him. I think I reached Jack."

"Then what's the big debate? I'm sure Colonel Smith won't waste the men's time if you didn't do any good today."

It wasn't very comforting, but it was probably true. Actually, by leaving it up to Colonel Smith, she was letting her own work be the judge. That appealed to her. It was settled.

Four

The Making of a
Silent Witness

In each of Nancy's six unsuccessful pregnancies, nausea had become the fabric of her day-to-day existence, broken only by episodes of violent vomiting and the periodic ordeal of choosing food. The nausea colored everything—everything except the shiny and wondrous expectation that at the end of the "ginger ale days" would be the miracle of her own child. She had to keep trying.

The first miscarriage was a profound disappointment. Sadness lingered for months, but there was still no reason to believe that she could not successfully bring a child to full term. With each successive miscarriage that hope faded and the sickness grew worse. Eventually the hemorrhaging became bad enough that her gynecologist, Dr. Charles Green, had advised her against allowing herself to become pregnant again. That's when she and John decided to adopt. The decision had closed a door on one of her

61

life's dreams.

Her opening, though, had made her wonder. In fact, from the thrilling, frightening, chaotic months that had followed her opening, two simple messages had emerged. They nagged at her.

Among the personages who represented themselves to Nancy in those early months were poets and scientists, some of whom Nancy and John were able to authenticate. But the most important to Nancy was Anna Dearworth, who had first contacted her through the Ouija. Although Anna had her hits and misses, she did better than most of the guides who swam in and out of Nancy's trances and automatic writing sessions. It was Anna who on June 8, 1973, told Nancy, "You will have a daughter one day...sometime within the next three years. You have seen her. She'll have happy hair. Name her Heidi Patrice." On December 28, 1974, Nancy wrote in a book of predictions: "Heidi comes next year."

But 1975 came and went and she did not become pregnant.

Now it was May of 1976. Nancy looked into her bathroom mirror. It had been six years since her last pregnancy, years that helped her deny the meaning of the nausea swimming within her. There had been other signs, but she had deflected them as well. At ballet class, where subtleties of form are hard to hide, she had noticed that her belly seemed to be bulging slightly, and earlier in the week, when she was with Sacco and Williams, her slacks had seemed uncomfortably tight. She had begun to diet, but even when she continued to gain weight, she refused to let her dream out of the box.

Tumor, she thought. She had better have it checked.

The next day Nancy found herself looking up at Dr. Green as he completed his internal examination and backed to the other side of the room. Stripping the rubber gloves off his hands, he said, "I have some good news and some bad news."

"Why are you over there?" she asked.

"Because when I tell you what's going on, you might kick me," he admitted.

"What are you talking about?" She was aware from his playful tone that it obviously wasn't cancer.

"You're pregnant."

The dream started to escape, but she stuffed it back. She would miscarry. She did not want another miscarriage.

"What's the good news?" she asked.

"That's the good news," Dr. Green said.

"And the bad news?"

"You're somewhere between two and a half and three months."

She understood instantly. Almost all of Nancy's miscarriages had occurred at three months. If she was going to miscarry, it would happen any day. There were signs that this time it might be different—signs she had ignored to keep her expectations in check. The nausea had started much later this time and it was periodic, not constant as it had been during her previous pregnancies.

Later, when her guard was down and these things swam into consciousness, Anna's messages came back to her. Then she recalled a conversation she had had in a Methodist church in Baltimore with a remarkable woman by the name of Olga Worrall.

When Nancy first opened in 1973, Olga already had an international reputation as a healer. Each month, hundreds of people from across the country would fill the sanctuary of the Mount Washington United Methodist Church in Baltimore and wait patiently for Olga or her team of trained healers to work on them. Stories of miraculous cures were not hard to come by at these services.

Nancy had heard of Olga through a magazine article, but it was not until John suggested that perhaps she could help Blake with his hyperactivity and learning disabilities that they made the first of what would become many Thursday morning trips from Newark to Baltimore to attend Worrall's service.

Nancy's first visit was magical. The parking lot was full of cars with license plates from all over the country. Inside, the sanctuary where the healer worked was nearly full. In the front, by the railing, stood Olga, a short, stout figure draped in a black minister's gown. From a distance she looked like everybody's grandmother. But when it was Nancy's turn to escort Blake to her, she felt the woman's commanding presence and warmth.

Olga seemed to Nancy especially drawn to the six-year-old, but Nancy wondered if this was part of her magic—the ability to create this rapport with everyone. Olga smiled down on the antsy youngster as Nancy recited Blake's diagnosed problems: hyperactivity, a midline perception deficiency, and other learning disabilities.

"And you're really naughty sometimes," Olga said to him conspiratorially.

Blake couldn't help but smile. "Yeah. I try to be good but I don't seem to be very good at it."

"Well," said Olga, "let's see what we can do about that."

She knelt down and wrapped her robed arms around him in a huge hug. Blake, who appeared half swallowed by some silken blackbird, looked helplessly up at his mother as if to ask, "What's this woman doing, Mom?"

No sooner had he looked up than he lost his balance. His arms flailed wildly until they locked roughly on Olga's shoulders. When she released him, Blake glared at her.

"What did you do to me?" he demanded.

Olga smiled and said, "I put a lot of nice stuff in you that will help you out."

Although Blake wasn't particular about the stuff he put in himself, he wasn't so sure about this strange lady's stuff.

As Travis watched Olga work on Blake, his color drained. Nancy worried that if Olga embraced *him* he might start crying, but the healer responded to his shyness in her calming tone with simple questions about his name and age. When he relaxed, she softly reached out and touched his arm. That was all.

When they returned to their seats, John took the boys out of the church to play. Nancy remained, waiting patiently for Olga. John, who was fond of lists, had prepared a lengthy one for Nancy. It contained all her ailments, which included allergies, asthma, colitis, and a back injury. The back injury had come in high school and at the time doctors thought it might eventually make her an invalid. They had offered her two options for relief from the constant and excruciating pain—surgery to cut nerves or pain-killing, addictive drugs. Nancy refused both and instead trained herself to use her mind to control the pain. In addition to prompting this early mental discipline, the injury may have had another effect. Some of Nancy's specialists blamed a leaking X-ray machine for Nancy's difficulty in bringing a child to full term.

When her turn came with Olga, Nancy was glad John had gone outside, because she had no intention of handing Olga a laundry list of maladies. She wanted to use her moments with this kindred soul to share her own conflict over the role she was being asked to take on. The episode that had brought her inner conflict to a head was the New Jersey case in which a young girl had been abducted, raped, and murdered, and her small body dumped by lonely railroad tracks. Nancy had correctly read the situation, including predicting that the girl would be found by a worker on a train. The girl had been Blake's age and reliving her murder had devastated Nancy.

But the incident was not the only thing troubling her. Her worldview was changing and with it many of her deeply felt assumptions and values. She was a traditional person, and the view society held of psychics was not lost on her.

She was surprised to find that this time when she approached the healer, the outpouring of love she felt was so pure, strong, and personal that tears welled up in her.

"Why are you crying?" Olga asked. Nancy told her about the missing child and the anguish of reliving her murder. She told of her opening and her confusion. She said she didn't know what to believe anymore, that she felt weird and isolated and wanted only to be normal.

"If you're weird, I'm weird, dearie," Olga said, stretching her robed arm to block filming by a camera crew. "Join the club. If God made you this way, this is what you have to do. And you'll have to find a way to adjust."

The trips to Baltimore became a monthly ritual for the Andersons, but it was not until their third visit that Olga asked why Nancy had adopted. Nancy explained the miscarriages. Without another word Olga walked over and put her hands on Nancy's stomach and back and said, "Well, let me fix that."

"Wait a minute," Nancy started to say. "It might damage the boys at this stage."

"Oh, come on, Mom," said Blake. "Have a baby. That would be so neat."

"Wouldn't that be neat," Olga said to Blake. "A little girl. You'll have a baby sister."

Blake was ecstatic.

It was on a subsequent visit, about a year before Nancy was even pregnant with Heidi, that Olga had confided to her that the child to be born to her would be blond and have blue eyes. "Those eyes," she had said, "there's something wrong with them but they can be fixed."

On the advice of Dr. Green, Nancy had quit working, dropped out of ballet, and spent her days coping with the nausea that was a constant reminder of past disappointments. The net effect of these precautions was isolation and boredom. Nancy hated it. Although she had been told to suspend her readings, when the phone rang and it was Smitty, she was grateful.

It had been two weeks since she and Williams and Sacco had visited Jack White, and she had convinced herself that the silence meant she was wrong. But in truth, the colonel could hardly be contained.

"You nailed that guard," he said. "Right down to his red hair and blue uniform."

"Guard?"

"At the arson site. You described an older man in a blue uniform, said he would be helpful. He isn't being very helpful yet, but they found him. Good work."

"Oh," said Nancy. "Thank you. I didn't know he was a guard."

"Lived on the site. We think he may have seen what happened the night of the fire," Smitty said. "Wish I could have been there when Williams knocked on his trailer door and this guy you described opens up."

"I don't think Sergeant Williams found me very helpful."

"Be patient, Nance. A few more hits like that and I won't be able to keep him off your back. He believes in getting the job done."

"Did they have any luck with the boy in the hospital?"

"That's what I'm calling about. I understand you have some pretty detailed descriptions of the assailants. I'd like to send a police artist over to do a sketch. Is that okay?"

"Well," she said, "I'm supposed to stay off duty for a while because I just discovered I'm pregnant."

"Pregnant?" Smitty broke in. "That's good news, for sure."

"I've been pregnant before and had trouble. A lot," she said.

"Well, that's a whole lot more important than anything else. Maybe this isn't such a good idea."

"No, you send him over. I can't see how talking to a police artist would be a problem."

Rolf Wysock was a towering man, so large that he had to have his uniforms custom made. Sacco accompanied him to Nancy's, enduring the complaints of another skeptic. Although Rolf didn't seem as irritated over the whole matter as Carl, he made it quite clear where he stood on matters psychic.

After a cordial introduction, Nancy said to Wysock, "You don't believe in all of this, do you?"

"No, I don't," he said with a slight German accent. He was a polite and sensitive man who got no pleasure from hurting someone else's feelings. But he also believed in speaking truthfully and bluntly.

Wysock had been raised in Germany by his grandparents. He had been thirteen when his grandmother died and he had left for Canada to live with his father. Only when his father drowned less than two years later did he finally return to Germany to live with his mother. But his relationship with his mother had been distant and the few years he had lived with her as a teenager did not heal the wounds. He had always been puzzled that one of his aunts had always seemed closer and more attentive to him than his own mother. But it was not until he was married and starting his own family that he entertained the idea that the woman he had thought was his mother all these years might not be. To find out, he and his wife journeyed to Canada and put the question directly to his aunt Liesellotte.

"Aunt Lilo," he said, "are you my mother?"

She was sandwiched between him and his wife. As the question crystallized between them, the color drained from the older woman's face and she began shaking and crying. When she finally had composed herself, she looked at the young man she had helped raise and said, "Please don't ask me that again. I can't answer you."

None of this was known to Nancy when she looked at her visitor and said, "You recently went looking for your mother."

Stunned, Wysock took refuge in his skepticism. "Well, I know my mother."

"No, you know the one who claims to be your mother."

"What?"

"Your mother's name is something like Elizabeth."

"My mother's name is Gertrude," protested Wysock.

"No," said Nancy. "It is my belief that your mother's name is something odd, but it's like Elizabeth."

Liesellotte is a derivative of Elizabeth.

Unnerved, Wysock shifted his attention to the work at hand. He showed Nancy his book of photographs. Altogether there were more than two hundred, and from them witnesses were asked to select eyes, noses, eyebrows, hair styles and such and then adjust the drawing as he blended them into a sketch.

As they worked, Nancy fended off Blake, who found anyone as big as Rolf worth checking out. Especially somebody that big who was a "drawer." When he was not pestering Rolf, he was trying to get Sacco to show him his gun.

As Rolf worked, he would once in a while ask Nancy if she had picked up anything else on him.

"You're going to make it very big," she said. "I see your name in an encyclopedia. And your son's."

When he completed the drawings, she looked at them, then closed her eyes to check them against her own vision and pronounced them finished.

At the door Rolf paused.

"How high will I go in the state police?" he asked.

"I see a star on your shoulder," she said.

Rolf laughed. "Now, I know you're wrong about that. We don't have generals in the state police."

"I see you in uniform and I see a star on your shoulder," was all she replied.

Seventeen years later, Rolf confided that what Nancy did not know at the time, and what he did not tell her, was that he was a member of the National Guard. Today he is a major and although the insignia is not a general's star, it looks very much like one.

After the visit from Wysock, the floodgates seemed to open. Calls started coming in two or three times a day. Usually they were from Greg Sacco, but sometimes they came from members of Carl's squad whom Nancy had not yet even met. The officers were often seeking elaboration on some bit of information that had been passed on from Greg or Carl. Greg often wanted to run a theory by her. If it was anybody but Greg, they all started out with the stiff and standard, "Carl Williams suggested I give you a call." But Carl Williams himself was never the caller.

"Are you sure they're white?" Greg asked one afternoon a couple of days after the visit from Wysock. She knew instantly the reference was to Jack White's assailants.

"No. I'm not sure of anything," Nancy admitted. "I've never done this before."

"Because we have a great suspect, in fact two. They come from the part of town you described. Both are violent, one a little more than the other. They fit your description, sort of. Their record fits what you said. But they're black."

"Remember when we were doing the composites with Wysock?" Nancy said. "We were trying to find a nose and the only one that matched was Negroid."

"So they could be blacks?" Greg suggested.

"I guess," Nancy said.

But before the suspects could be approached, Sacco made a startling discovery.

"You know those drawings Wysock did?" he asked a couple of days later. "I took them over to the high school. We got positive IDs on both: they're good friends of Jack's and they were at the gas station the night of his assault. But earlier. How do you figure that?"

When it came to her psychic gifts, Nancy was only learning how to figure anything. She asked and the images came. How she had accurately described two of Jack's best friends instead of his assailants was a mystery. And Greg said they were good likenesses, so close that the first person he showed the drawings to identified them by name.

"You don't suppose they did it, do you?" she asked.

"Airtight alibis," Greg said.

While Nancy enjoyed working with Greg, it bothered her that Carl wouldn't get on the phone with her. Instead, Greg made the calls and Carl would fire his questions through him.

"Why don't you ask her yourself?" she heard Greg say one day while fielding a call from the barracks. "You know what's going on here, don't you, Nancy?"

"Yeah, Carl's too chicken to get on the phone and ask me questions," Nancy said.

Greg burst into laughter as he turned to Carl. "You should hear what she said about you, Carl."

"What?" Even off the phone, Nancy could hear him.

"She says you're too chicken to get on the phone and ask her your own questions."

There was a long silence, broken by a gruff "Hello."

Nancy's delight at getting the best of the skeptic was short-lived. If Williams's men *questioned* witnesses, Williams himself grilled them. He would ask a question and then question each word of the answer. His style was not entirely designed to aggravate, although that was its chief effect.

"This smell, at the arson site, you said it was kerosene, but gasoline too. Which was it?"

"Both."

"How could it be both? Gasoline doesn't smell like kerosene."

"I mean each."

"Which each?"

"Both each."

"You mean this guy couldn't make up his mind, so he threw kerosene and gasoline on the fire?"

"I mean I smelled both."

"At the same time?"

"No, time isn't important when I range. Things overlap."

"But smells don't?"

"Don't what?"

"Overlap?"

"No, it's more like they're side by side."

"You mean events get all mixed together, but smells don't?"

"Not mixed together; the sequence gets mixed up."

And so it went, endlessly. Carl's hunger for detail was unquenchable. He wanted license numbers and vehicle numbers. When she described the fire starters, providing what she thought were very detailed physical descriptions, he asked for their names, which she didn't get. Failing that, he wanted their addresses.

"I can't give you the guy's address," she would say.

"Oh?" Carl would respond, as if to ask, "Then why am I doing this?"

When she got off the phone from these conversations she felt angry and useless, but she could not point to a single rude thing that Carl Williams had done.

For his part, Williams was actually growing to like Nancy in spite of himself. Maybe it was the way she liked to play gotcha, or maybe it was her sincerity. Williams was ordinarily wary of people who wanted to help. He knew well that for some unfathomable reason people liked to get next to troopers. It must be a tiny bit like what actors go through, he thought to himself. But he had become convinced that this wasn't what Nancy was about. She wasn't just trying to latch on, as he called it.

Her instinct to help seemed genuine. In fact, he felt a little sorry for her. *How can she believe this crap?* he asked himself. *She looks perfectly normal, she speaks normally. How can she believe it?*

And yet, though her IDs in the Jack White case had proved wrong, they had been real people—people known to Jack and people who had been at the station the night he was assaulted. How to account for that?

What a lot of people didn't realize about Carl Williams was that behind his no-nonsense demeanor was a mind more open than most. Zero-based thinking, he called it. It was what enabled him to stand at a blackboard in front of his men and run through the possibilities of a homicide, however absurd they seemed, as if each was actually the way it had happened.

He had found that only that kind of openness generated the connections that solved murders. He had also learned that keeping rolling was often the most important thing. Turning over the rocks. Sooner or later something would connect, as if the intensity of the search alone would squeeze leads out of thin air.

And thin air was all they had on Jack White—thin air and a page-and-a-half police report. The lack of leads made Nancy's IDs seem like gold. When they fell through, Williams went back to squeezing thin air in brainstorming sessions that could occur anywhere. Sometimes they were at his house, where he and Sacco returned religiously every day so that Carl could smear peanut butter on Saltines and brainstorm with *McHale's Navy* as background noise. Other sessions took place on the phone, which frequently seemed to Carl's wife, Kitty, to be an outgrowth of her husband's ear. Sacco's wife, Marsha, a close friend of Kitty's, would often complain that Greg would come home from ten- or twelve-hour days only to spend another two hours on the phone with Carl.

The other place brainstorming occurred was in Carl's den.

It was several weeks after their initial meeting that Nancy received her first invitation to one of these sessions.

Before Nancy broke the ice, Greg had made the calls to Nancy for Carl when they were at work. When Carl got an idea at home, he would have his wife call. This perplexed Kitty, since Carl had never before been bashful about using the telephone. In fact, he was a self-described "phone blabberer." Nancy—who, Carl soon found out, was a phone blabberer too—especially enjoyed the calls from Kitty.

From the outset they had hit it off. Both were bright mothers who were equally comfortable talking books, babies, or bad guys. In fact, once she found out Nancy was pregnant, Kitty didn't wait for questions from Carl to check on how her new friend was doing. But Nancy's first invitation to a brainstorming session at the Williamses' home was engineered by Kitty, who was growing weary of acting as go-between. One question would have been all right, but the back-and-forth grilling was too much. "Why don't you just come over and then they can ask you themselves," she suggested.

The idea of facing the whole squad froze Nancy. "Oh, I wouldn't mind but I've got these little monsters," she said.

"Connie can watch them," Kitty said, referring to her daughter.

"I'm not sure I can find you," she said.

"Tell her we'll come and get her," Carl said after Kitty relayed the excuse.

When they arrived at the Williamses', Blake left little doubt about how he had been talked into coming. Dressed in a bathing suit and flip flops, he had flippers tucked under one arm, a snorkel and mask parked on his forehead. In one hand he had his rolled-up

jeans and in the other a towel. "Where's the pool?" he asked before
they had even gotten through the door. Everyone but Travis
laughed out loud. "Blake!" said his younger brother. "That's
rude."

"What?" Blake asked.

"This way," said Kitty as she led the procession through the
kitchen and down two steps into a carpeted room with green
paneling and a built-in cherry bookcase on the far wall. It was a
cozy room. Scattered about were a small sofa, a couple of chairs,
and half a dozen detectives. Nancy's gaze went immediately to the
holstered guns parked next to each of the men. She immediately
glanced at Blake, but he was distracted by the sidearms only
briefly. "This isn't the pool," Blake protested.

"This way, Blake," Kitty said as she led him back up through the
kitchen and out into the backyard. Nancy excused herself and
followed, not comfortable to send Blake off until she had gotten
the lay of the land for herself. Then too, she had found all those
men and their guns disconcerting. She was not much calmed by
the sight of the Williamses' twenty-by-forty-foot in-ground pool.
All she could think of was, *Blake's going to drown something. I
know it.* When Carl introduced the boys to Smokey, she had an
idea of what.

Smokey was the Williamses' Samoyed, a medium-sized dog with
a characteristic ruff of hair framing his huskylike face. He relished
licking kids, and the force of Smokey's tongue was all Blake
needed to feign a fall into the pool. Wet at last, he would, Nancy
hoped, calm down.

She followed Kitty and Carl back into the den. Travis, who was
playing ball with Smokey, quickly gave up his game and tagged
along back inside with the adults. When they were all settled,
Nancy found herself sitting with Travis on the sofa. Directly in
front of her sat Williams, clearly in command from his swivel
rocker. He was flanked by most of his squad, who seemed restless
to get beyond the chitchat and back to work. Carl accommodated
by asking Nancy how she had screwed up so badly on the Jack

White IDs.

Nancy was tense but expert at hiding it—a fringe benefit of her meditation skills. She let a flash of anger pass and said, "Did I? Greg said they ended up being real people. And you know we never did draw the third person."

"No witness credibility after the first two were wrong," said Carl.

"Not wrong, exactly," said Greg. "Dead ringers for two of his friends."

"The right answer to the wrong question," observed George Patterson. Nancy had talked to Patterson on the phone but had not met him until tonight. She read George as probably the brightest of the group in pure intellect but not as streetwise as some of the other squad members. Like Greg he was fascinated with Nancy's abilities and among the most willing to utilize them.

"That's what I'm saying," Nancy went on. "You're thinking about this as if I'm a normal witness because that's what you're used to. But maybe that's the error. You ask a question, I get an image, but maybe the image isn't always literal. And maybe it answers a question you haven't asked. "

"Maybe it's wrong too," said Jack Mayer. Mayer was a big man who prided himself on being a curmudgeon. He was a tough, skeptical, streetwise cop, as focused on clearing cases as Williams. When Carl had introduced Nancy to him earlier, she had tried to break the ice by pointing out the similarity between his name and her maiden name—Myer. Jack had just looked at her as if waiting for the point.

"Let' s not be like all the other monkeys," said Carl. "Even if it's not right, if it keeps us rolling, it could lead to something."

Nancy was surprised to hear what could pass as support coming from the swivel rocker.

"Anything on Jack White would be very welcome right now," Greg added.

Williams's assessment of the case from the beginning had been that if the assailant was a transient, the only way they'd get him was if he was caught for something else and somebody did a deal with him. But if he was local, Williams had no doubt they'd get him. The fact that Nancy saw three assailants inclined him to believe it was local, since transients don't usually travel in packs. The other connection it made for him was to a local burglary ring that at that time was hitting supermarkets. But since the IDs were wrong, he didn't know where to take her information next.

"You guys have to remember, this is uncharted territory for me," said Nancy.

"That *is* the problem," Patterson said. "How does it work?"

"I'm not sure it always works the same way," explained Nancy. "I think sometimes what I get is literal and sometimes it's symbolic. And I can't always tell which."

"It didn't seem very symbolic at the Gulf station," Greg pointed out. "You looked like you were in trouble."

"That was a new one for me. Apparently, the scene *can* overwhelm me."

"Overwhelm you?" Patterson asked.

Nancy wasn't sure she herself understood, but she had given it a lot of thought and decided to take a stab at an explanation. "Events, at least highly charged events like Jack White's beating, must leave a residue of some kind that I can pick up on. I think it's emotional, because I always feel something. I may or may not get images. Sometimes I get smells, sometimes sounds. Sometimes it's not sensory. I just become aware of stuff. Information."

"But you have to be at the site?" Greg asked.

"Apparently not," she finally said after running her experiences in her mind. "I wasn't at the site of the houseboat accident where that Cilimburg boy drowned, but when I stood on the bank and ranged it in my mind, it was like I was with him that night. It was as real as my experience at the Gulf station."

"Ranged it?" Patterson repeated.

"That's what I call focusing or tuning in to something. It can be a person, a photo, a crime scene. I focus and open and information comes to me."

"So what are you saying?" Carl pressed her.

"I guess I can trigger it by going to the scene or by simply focusing on the person involved." She paused for a moment. "It does seem more manageable from a distance. I have more control. There's a difference in intensity."

"Well, if you can get all that, why can't you give me serial numbers, names, and license plates?" Carl demanded.

"Because then she'd put you out of a job," said Kitty.

"That's okay, I'll just take her to Delaware Park and live the good life," her husband replied.

"Oh no," Kitty shot back. "She's already agreed to go to the track with *me*."

During one of their telephone chats, Nancy had told Kitty about the time her grandfather had taken her to a racetrack. She was very young, maybe nine. But by going down in the paddock she had been able to empathize with the horses and jockeys and successfully pick winners. It had only happened twice. Her grandmother, Emma Myer—the powerful matriarch of the Myer family—had nearly burst an artery screaming at Ellis when she discovered where he had been taking their granddaughter.

"But Em, she loves animals," she recalled him protesting.

"Then take her to the zoo," Emma snapped as she hustled Nancy out of the room.

The Myers had always possessed a unique rapport with animals. Nancy's father had it, and several of her Myer great-uncles had been animal trainers and drivers at harness racing tracks. Whether she herself could pick winners at the track she had no idea, but maybe after twenty years the frightening effect of Gran's admonition had worn off.

"Okay," said Carl. "Kitty's taking bets."

"Oh no," Nancy protested, "I don't mind picking horses, but I'd be a nervous wreck if I thought somebody was actually *betting* on them."

"You want to pick horses just for fun?" Mayer said in disbelief.

Even Nancy had to laugh when she thought about how her

proposition must have hit the men around her.

"What *can* you do to show us how you work, Nancy?" asked Patterson.

"Do you have somebody you would like me to describe? Somebody I've never met?"

"Hawk," said Carl. He was the only member of the unit not present.

"Hawk? That's his name?" said Nancy.

"Hawkinson, Ted Hawkinson," said Kitty.

Nancy smiled. As soon as the name was out of Kitty's mouth, she was looking at an image of a court jester. She smiled. "He makes you laugh. Always pulling practical jokes. Lightens things up." She looked directly at Jack Mayer as she said it. Smiles popped out all around.

Hawkinson was exactly as Nancy had described. He was a well-rounded cop who was just as comfortable wrestling a drunk out of a bar as conducting an investigation. But his defining trait was his love of jokes, practical and otherwise.

One time while on dispatch he had called a rookie trooper in early and explained he wanted the trooper to go ahead of the shift to the Drum & Ale bar and order five large pizzas so when the men got there they wouldn't have to wait. Grateful for being called in early, he was happy to comply. Word had it that the trooper was selling substantially discounted pizza by the slice around the bar while the shift partied elsewhere that night.

"Renfro," Mayer offered.

"He just went through an operation that wasn't necessary and it didn't work out very well," Nancy said. "The operation was okay, but for some reason you guys needled him about it endlessly."

"Okay," said Carl, "which one of you guys told her about his hair transplant?"

A new wave of laughter filled the room.

And so the evening went. Kitty kept ducking out by the pool to check on the kids or refill the pretzels and potato chips. Travis would periodically tug at his mother's shirt to advise her that he was sure Blake was causing some sort of ruckus out back. Carl would frequently pull out of the discussion to answer the phone on the table beside his chair. While he handled the call, the work stopped, replaced by chitchat and bargaining with Nancy over her escalating cut if only she would take them to the track.

Mayer took advantage of one of these lulls to raise a question about the arson that had been bothering all of them. Street sources had corroborated Nancy's reading that several pieces of equipment had been hidden at a warehouse the suspect owned in Rehoboth, but their sources weren't strong enough for a search warrant. How could they get on that property? Nobody had ever heard of a warrant being issued on the basis of a psychic impression.

Ideas were batted about, but nothing that seemed practical emerged. When Carl returned they told him what they had been discussing. He shrugged, then seemed to get an idea. "Maybe," was all he said.

Nancy was the first to leave. Travis had fallen asleep against her and even Blake had tired himself out showing off for Connie. Nancy felt good about the evening. Though she'd been terrified at first, somewhere between the horse races and the hair transplant, barriers had come down. She felt she had become a person to them. Maybe she had even become a good sport.

A few days later, in the afternoon, Nancy answered her phone only to be greeted by gales of laughter. She was about to hang up when she recognized Greg's voice trying first to squelch his own laughter, then to quiet others behind him.

"Hello?" she said.

"Nance, I'm sorry, I can't stop laughing," he explained. "We just got back from executing the warrants on the arson and I think we finally made a believer out of Carl."

"Oh," Nancy said.

"The guy owns a car dealership in Rehoboth, and guess what we found in one of his warehouses?"

"Three pieces of farm equipment, which were supposed to be

melted scrap iron."

"That's not all. Dead ringers for the two fire starters you described. They work for the guy."

Nancy was delighted but puzzled. "How did you end up establishing probable cause to get the warrants?" she asked.

"That's the best part," Greg continued. "It was Carl's idea. He told the judge he had a witness."

"Nobody mentioned that the other night. *Do* you?"

"Sort of," he said.

"Anybody I gave you?"

Greg couldn't suppress his laughter any longer. "I guess so," he said. "It's you."

Five

Just Stay Out
of the House

Mary Amelia Allen lived alone in a trim, neatly
kept bungalow with an immaculate yard and roses that were the
envy of the neighborhood. Her house was on Governor Printz
Boulevard in Claymont, a residential community north of
Wilmington where violent crime was a rarity. In the two years
following the death of her husband, she had settled into an
ordinary routine not uncommon for a seventy-three-year-old
widow. Each morning Mary would ride the 9:30 bus into
Wilmington, get off on Market Street, and walk to LeRoy's
Feminine Fashions, where she was one of their best salespeople.
Each afternoon she would return home at precisely 5:40 P.M.

Mary was a diminutive, soft-spoken person well liked by
workers and customers alike. But once home, except for frequent
visits by her three grown children, she kept to herself, rarely
talking to anyone. When she did, the subject was inconsequential

81

small talk, more often than not the weather. She was a trusting person, and she rarely locked the doors when she was home.

On the morning of Friday, July 24, 1975, coworkers became worried when Mary failed to arrive at the shop on time. As the day passed without word, they called the house, but there was no answer. With growing apprehension they tracked down a relative by calling all the Allens in the phone book. It was afternoon by the time they reached the home of Ralph, one of her two sons. Ralph's wife Margaret drove immediately to Claymont.

In the bedroom of the meticulously kept house that to Margaret had always represented neatness and order, she found something that rocked her, as it would soon rock the community of Claymont. In the otherwise tidy bedroom, on a bed drenched in blood, lay the body of her mother-in-law, lifeless and riddled with over seventy stab wounds.

By late July of 1976 Nancy was unable to work every day. Kitty and members of Carl's unit—many of whom had become a rooting squad for her pregnancy—kept Carl apprised of Nancy's availability. So when he called for help on the brutal murder just handed to him by Smitty, he was relieved to hear a chipper Nancy answer the phone. Working in his favor were the weather—a brilliant summer day with low humidity and a cloudless blue sky— and Nancy's boredom at being homebound.

As with most of their cases, the Mary Allen case was a year old and had long ago hit a dead end. He could tell Nancy that it was a murder but nothing else, not even the victim's name.

When working from photos she required only the name. An alternate method they had worked out put Nancy within visual range of the scene. For this method she was told nothing. Carl wanted her to do readings at actual crime scenes, but after the experience at the Gulf station, Nancy refused. She had to get enough distance from the experience to report it rather than be mauled by it.

Carl preferred the scene to photos because it seemed to him a more logical way to work. Nancy smiled to herself that he was more comfortable with a reading derived from the emotional residue of a murder scene than one coming from a photographic image. But she understood how he felt. Somehow being near the scene made the crime more tangible. The method had a more practical benefit as well. Carl preferred not telling Nancy anything about the murder. If he told her nothing, he ruled out the possibility of her impressions coming from something she had heard or read. Carl was also able to use whatever details he had on the case to gauge whether she was on track or not. Neither knew enough about how her ability worked to be sure that a fact from Nancy matching a fact from their own investigation meant everything else was accurate, but it raised Carl's comfort level.

Today Nancy was mildly surprised to see two unmarked cars pull up outside her house within an hour of Carl's call; she judged this must be a priority case that the colonel wanted quick closure on. They drove north on 95, but once they exited the expressway above Wilmington, she got lost in the twists and turns of residential neighborhoods. Carl brought her up-to-date on the arson case, which looked like it would be going to trial, and the Jack White case, which was going nowhere.

"Except that song," Carl said, suddenly remembering some-thing Greg had told him. "That song about the bird."

"Fly, Robin, Fly," Nancy prompted.

"Greg talked to the mother and it turns out she's nuts about that song. Bought the record, in fact, something she never does."

Nancy listened for some sign that Carl might be impressed, but after a minute passed and no one had spoken, he merely said, "I guess a lot of people like that song."

When they finally jerked to a stop, they were in front of a cute little brick house with a porch and a trellis up one side.

For a moment she thought this was the site, but Carl excused himself, saying only that he had an errand to run and that he would be just a minute. This kind of detour was not unusual. Detectives often touch base with several investigations in a single day and Carl

rarely offered an explanation for his actions. Nancy never asked.
She felt it would breach some sort of police protocol.

He and the detectives from the other car walked into the house
as if it were vacant. After ten or so minutes, Nancy was beginning
to worry that she would need a bathroom before they returned. It
was also getting hot. Her patience was growing thin when one of
the detectives returned to the car and apologized for the delay.

"It must be hot in there," he said. "Why don't you come inside.
We're just checking a few things and then we'll be gone."

Nancy was grateful. She followed him across the porch and into
a hallway. His back and that hallway are where her recollection of
the interior of the Mary Allen house ended. *Upon her entering the
house, terrified, angry screams and a blinding white light engulfed
her. She reeled from the impact. Nausea surged within her as a heavy
weight descended upon her chest.*

*"GET OUT GET OUT GET OUT!" a woman screamed in a
raspy voice full of rage. Nancy tried to locate it, but within the
blinding whiteness, directions were meaningless. Dazed, she bumped
into something soft. A person?*

*From a long distance, barely audible through the screams, she
heard, "Are you all right?"*

"GET OUT GET OUT GET OUT!"

*"Overheated. I think I'm going to throw up," she found herself
saying.*

"GET OUT GET OUT GET OUT!"

"Why don't you go outside and get some air."

"GET OUT GET OUT GET OUT!"

*She could not find the door. She couldn't even find the door she had
just walked through.*

"GET OUT GET OUT GET OUT!"

*Men were trying to talk to her, but they were far away and hard to
hear. Farther than before. Her own voice seemed to be suddenly
locked. She had to get out. Something awful was going to happen if
she didn't get out.*

"GET OUT GET OUT GET OUT!"

She felt faint. Spinning.

"GET OUT GET OUT GET OUT!"

Then a hand on her elbow. Guided. Someone had taken hold of her and was walking her out of the house. She stumbled the few short steps back to the porch and then walked on to the squad car. Putting her head in her hands she tried to clear the woman's anguish from her mind and body, but the screams would not subside.

Carl sauntered over to the car and asked casually, "What's up?"

He had tricked Nancy into entering the house and she had reacted violently. But he still wasn't ready to acknowledge that her swoon was anything but histrionics. Maybe hormones from the pregnancy. Maybe the heat or a smell in the stuffy, closed-up house. Never would he have guessed the answer he got.

"Get out. Mary says get out of the house," Nancy said. "And you get me out of here."

"Who?" A chill ran through Carl.

"Mary. Her name is Mary."

Carl was beginning to be impressed. He wasn't sure he believed in emotional residue and he sure didn't believe in ghosts, but whatever source had provided Nancy with that name might provide other information. He wanted more.

"Get back in there," he said. "Tell Mary I want to know who killed her. I want to know what they said, I want to know what they did. If Mary is going to talk to you, let's get something good out of Mary."

"Mary wants you out of the house. I wouldn't go back in there. She said to get out." The screams still rang in her ears.

"Nancy, we're the police; we don't go out, we go in."

"Not there," Nancy said.

"Look, Nancy, I don't know everything that's possible. But if this is happening, great. What better witness than the victim? Tell me about it."

Nancy was adamant. She had felt Mary's terror deep in her own soul and now believed that even here, outside the house, she was in danger. They were all in danger. The entity she was hearing was panicked, and furiously angry. Hatred and rage poured from her.

"Get me out of here," she told Carl.

Carl looked heavenward. "Can we work it somewhere else?"

"Just get me out of here. Now."

Carl gave the signal and the squad members piled back into their cars and drove until the screaming in her head subsided. Carl pulled into the first available driveway and the other car followed. The detectives from the other car piled around to listen.

"Well, what did you learn?"

"Never to trust a cop," Nancy said. A ripple of amusement passed through the assembled detectives.

Nancy then proceeded to describe the killer in stunning detail. Carl immediately knew whom she was referring to. Even though he had just gotten the case, one suspect had jumped out from the beginning. He asked for more. She described the relationship between the killer and the victim and gave them a motive.

"She knew him. They argued—a hateful argument. In fact, the whole murder was hateful. It was overkill. He just kept stabbing and stabbing and stabbing to degrade her."

Carl nodded to himself. Although Nancy didn't know it, the body had been punctured with seventy-three stab wounds.

"He's brilliant and angry and very disturbed," Nancy said. "Oh." She blinked and shook her head as if she were trying to tune in a radio broadcast. "He's a shoplifter."

She had no idea why that was important. It seemed a small thing in the context of this mutilation murder, but it had just been shoved on her and she had learned not to do a lot of editing of the information she received.

She continued, "He left you clues. He's challenging you."

"What do you mean? What clues?"

"He left something right in the middle of the floor. Right in the middle and it was missed. And it was a very direct clue," she said.

Carl pulled out photographs of the scene and handed them to Nancy.

"Here, the kitchen," she said after reviewing them. "Here's where it was."

Carl took the photo and gazed at a section of empty kitchen floor.

She continued flipping through the stack, stopping at a picture of a teacup in a saucer sitting on the counter. She lightly ran her fingers over the image and said with assurance, "That's one of the clues too."

She leafed through the photographs but always came back to the kitchen. "Some things have been moved which shouldn't have been moved," she said. "And there's something in the middle of the floor that's important." Carl looked back at the photo he had been holding.

"Nancy, there's nothing there. Is that the clue—nothing?"

Nancy shrugged. She didn't know.

It was not long before Carl did.

He decided to take Nancy's information to Margaret Allen. As the first person at the scene, perhaps she saw something that would explain the importance of the teacup and the missing clue from the kitchen floor.

Explaining Nancy to people was never easy for Carl. He had not quite come up with a satisfactory generic term for her and he hesitated to use *psychic* because it had, well, connotations.

When he met with Margaret Allen, he just said they had reason to believe that these two pictures were important, and he showed her the photos of the teacup and the kitchen floor.

"You were the first person on the scene," he said. "Do you remember anything being here on the floor?"

Mrs. Allen got quiet for a moment. She seemed upset. "When I came in the house that day there was a grocery bag on the floor. I noticed it because it was so unlike Mary to leave something like that out of place," she said. "She just didn't do it. And then when I looked in the bag and saw it was a bag of marshmallows, I knew it wasn't hers."

"How so?"

"She was diabetic," said Mrs. Allen. "She would never allow anything with sugar in it in the house."

"So you took the bag and showed it to the officers?"

"Oh no, I wouldn't touch anything. The officer moved it," Mrs. Allen said. "I didn't think that was a good idea. But he just grabbed it and put it on the counter."

Carl shook his head. Even this civilian knew better than to move things at a crime scene. "How about this one?" He showed her the picture of the teacup.

"Well," said Mrs. Allen, "Mary would never have left it out on the counter. She would have immediately washed it out and put it in the drain board."

Carl looked back at the photo.

"Was your mother-in-law right-handed?"

Mrs. Allen nodded and asked to see the photo again. "Oh, of course. The handle is on the left and the spoon is on the left. Somebody else used that cup."

Carl went to Troop 2 angry at their slipshod investigation. His opinion of their work did not improve when one of the original investigators told him no significant evidence had been found at the scene. Although there was considerable animosity toward Carl's special investigations unit throughout the state police, it was especially rabid at Troop 2. Carl wasn't sure why, but he felt it relieved him of whatever small obligation he might have ordinarily felt to be tactful.

"What the hell is this?" he asked, pointing to a photograph of the marshmallows.

"Marshmallows," said the investigator.

"Since the victim was a diabetic, she didn't eat marshmallows, so where did they come from?"

"We don't know," the man said, suddenly stiff.

"Where's the murder weapon?"

After a pause, the man said, "We didn't determine one."

Carl showed him a picture of a knife found in a flower bed behind the garage about a week after the murder.

"What's this?" he asked.

"That's a knife we found, but you can't assume that was the murder weapon."

"That's why you never had prints taken?"

The investigator shrugged.

"The medical examiner can match that blade up with the wounds to the centimeter," Carl said.

The investigator said nothing.

Carl was still fuming when he entered the evidence room and was given a huge box containing many of the items pictured in the photographs. A neatly folded quilt stained with blood was squeezed in with a brown grocery bag, the teacup, and the knife, among other items.

Carl lifted the bag of rock-hard marshmallows out and examined it. He thought for a moment, gazing at the misshapen white candy, and then fished his hand back into the grocery bag. When he pulled it out, a sales slip dangled precariously between two fingers. He recognized the name of the store. It was in the Concord Mall, which was not along the bus line Mrs. Allen normally took to work. Given that she was diabetic and that she would have had to go out of her way to buy the marshmallows, it seemed a pretty safe bet that somebody else had brought them into the house. Considering Nancy's impression that they were a significant clue, Carl's bet was the killer.

He signed out the knife and the sales slip. The knife's serial number went to the manufacturer and the knife itself went to the medical examiner, who easily identified it as the murder weapon. Carl himself went to the Concord Mall. Carl took the receipt and a photograph of his prime suspect along with photos of other men. As he had hoped, the manager was able to trace the clerk who had rung up the sale a year before. That clerk turned out to have an impressive memory. It helped that the customer she found among Carl's photos was strange and had often hassled her.

"How was he strange?" Carl asked.

"He just seemed funny," she said. "He would complain about

shelves not being neat. He would get really worked up over it, then just smile and like laugh at himself. Strange."

"Anything else?"

"Well," she hesitated, looking back and forth between Carl and the manager. "I was never sure, but I think he was stealing."

"Stealing?"

"You know, shoplifting. But I could never catch him. And to tell you the truth, I don't think I would have confronted him anyway."

"Why not?" Carl asked.

The clerk seemed embarrassed. "He scared me," she said.

"Does he still come in?"

"No. I haven't seen him for a long time, maybe a year." Then she added, "And I'm glad."

The evidence against Carl's suspect continued to accumulate, but it was all suggestive, not conclusive. The murder weapon turned out to be a promotional knife given out by Acme Markets. Tens of thousands of them had been distributed. The suspect's mother shopped at Acme—suggestive, but hardly conclusive. Carl's background check turned up minor incidents in which the suspect had struck out at people who had made him angry, deflating tires or slashing screens. He also had a neatness fetish; everything had to be spotlessly clean. That could explain why the scene had been tidied up.

But without physical evidence or a confession tying him to the murder, Carl knew they had no case.

"Why don't you ask Mary who the hell did it?" he would say to Nancy.

"She won't tell me, Carl."

"Why not? I'm her buddy."

"She just wants you to stay out of her house," Nancy said.

Carl cupped his hand around his mouth and said to the ceiling of his den, "Yo, Mary, just say this guy's name and I'm gone."

But Mary was silent on who had killed her—or mostly silent. Almost from the day Nancy visited the house, incidents started occurring that were becoming hard to ignore. Even Carl had witnessed them.

Among Carl's investigative techniques was to sit at the scene of a crime and let ideas run through his head. He would do this at any time of the day or night, by himself or with whatever detective was available. He had found the Allen house an ideal spot for such noodling. Nancy had disagreed and warned Carl to stay clear. Most of the squad heeded her warning, but not Carl. Now he was sitting in the driveway of the house at dusk. His partner was edgy.

"Does it make any sense that Mary wouldn't want us to solve her murder?" he reasoned.

"You heard Nancy. Mary's irrational about it," came the reply.

"Look, if somebody killed *me*, I wouldn't go chasing *you* away if you were trying to find out who did it."

They were parked about fifty feet or so from the kitchen window. Suddenly the detective cut Carl's assurances short with screams of, "There she is! There she is!"

"Christ!" protested Carl.

"There. In the window, I saw her," said the detective.

"Who?" Carl asked.

"Mary," his partner screamed.

"Cut me some slack. We're not here to upset you, we're here to get something to upset that sonofabitch that killed her. Now get with the program."

"She was there. I saw her in the window." The detective ignored Carl's glare. "And Carl, she looked pissed."

"Okay, if you saw somebody in the house, I have a key, let's go in and investigate. Nobody's supposed to be in that house, least of all Mary."

"You're crazy, Williams. You go. I'm not going."

"Okay," said Carl. "Let's look around the outside then."

The two detectives walked around back, where Carl noticed an old leather mail pouch lying on the ground. It was the style often used by bankers. Both men were surprised they hadn't noticed it before. Time and weather had beaten it partly into the ground.

But Carl, being the more experienced of the two officers,

allowed the younger man to pick it up. No sooner had he peeled it off the ground than an angry swarm of bees rushed out at him and sent both detectives flying for the car.

Inside, with the windows cranked up, all Carl could hear was the smacking sound of hand against flesh and constant shouting, "Mary did it, Mary did it!" He was too busy swatting bees himself to argue. When the last bee fell to the floor, they assessed the damage. Carl had escaped with a couple of bites, but his partner was peppered and beginning to swell. Carl took him back to his own car so he could drive to the emergency room.

When Carl returned home, he found Nancy and Kitty sitting in the den chatting. "What happened to you?" Kitty asked.

"Mary did it," Carl said.

"What?" Nancy asked.

"That's what some people think because a psychic I know put it in their heads," he said. "I think some damned bees did it."

"I can fix that," Nancy said. And she proceeded to hold her hand just above the bites and close her eyes. Much to Carl's surprise, the bee stings quit hurting.

Carl was not the only officer to have trouble at the Mary Allen house. On one visit Wysock, the police artist, got only a couple of feet into the house when he ripped his uniform and gashed his arm on a nail protruding from the molding. Another officer slipped on the stairs and twisted his ankle. Nancy argued that Mary was a force to be reckoned with and that they should respect her wishes and stay out of the house.

Though Carl wasn't convinced that Mary truly roamed the halls of her old house, he considered capitalizing on the reputation the house was developing by trying to spook the murderer into a confession. Reasoning that his prime suspect was local and intimately aware of Mary's habits, his plan was to put the lights on a timer that would match Mary's old routine and dress a policewoman up in some of Mary's old clothes. She would roam the house at night, in the hope that the murderer would drive by and catch a glimpse of what might seem to him an apparition.

When he told Nancy of his plan, she nearly flipped.

"Carl, you can't have somebody in there messing with Mary's electric. Or dressing in Mary's clothes. That's begging for trouble."

The Delaware attorney general came to the same conclusion, but for different reasons, and Carl decided their best shot was an interrogation in which they would confront their suspect with their strong circumstantial case and hope he would break.

Carl was an expert interrogator. He knew where he wanted to get and patiently worked his way there, skillfully mixing chitchat with questions that moved the interview forward. His feedback came from eyes, gestures, and tone of voice. He would constantly recast his questions to keep the suspect comfortable, to avoid spooking him. Hours would pass in this tedious process before the suspect would say anything useful. But in the end it was worth it. Carl hated convictions without confessions and it was rare that he had to settle for them.

But his suspect in the Mary Allen case was not typical. Carl had had him in for an interview several times, had worked him with the deft touch of a diamond cutter, and yet when he raised the hammer for the business stroke, the suspect would look at him with hurt, earnest eyes and say, "I don't know why you think I did this. How can I convince you I didn't?" And they would be back at the beginning.

Finally, out of desperation, he decided to try an unorthodox technique. Though no one knew exactly what Nancy was capable of or how she did what she did, it seemed clear that she was quite good at tapping into the minds of suspects. Why not hook her up by radio to Carl during an interrogation and let her provide input on the suspect's thinking? Nancy loved the idea. It seemed an ideal use of her abilities.

That's how Carl's squad came to be stringing cable through the crawl space above the drop ceiling at Troop 6 one hot August afternoon. Carl supervised and Greg, who had an engineering background, was the technical consultant. Around them, permanent workers complained that the renovations were sucking all the cool air into the rafters. Carl would admonish them for letting a petty thing like their comfort interfere with *real* police work.

Nancy, Patterson, Mayer, Hawkinson, and Sacco would be stationed in a room safely distant from the interrogation room. There they could watch the questioning on a video monitor and make notes on the suspect's responses. If they detected a discrepancy in the answers or noticed something which contradicted some factual evidence one of them had uncovered, they could communicate that to Carl over a shared microphone. His receiver was mounted behind one ear, like a hearing aid. Nancy was to watch for lies. Lies caused a person's aura—an energy halo that surrounds the physical body—to go from layers of color to gray. Other kinds of emotional stress also caused alterations in the aura, so she hoped to be able to cue Carl when he was pushing a hot button.

Chief among their concerns was that Nancy not be seen and possibly recognized by the suspect. They feared that recognizing her might spook him into withdrawing from the interview or worse, prompt him to target Nancy.

When Nancy arrived, it was still daylight. She parked her Ford and walked into the barracks. The room was electric. No single thing cued her, just a feeling in the air. She found it amplified her own anxieties. The desk officer asked for her name, though he seemed to know immediately who she was, then made a call. Soon Sacco emerged from a solid-looking steel door.

"Let's hustle back," he said. "Our man just took a bathroom break and we don't want you to run into him."

The building was low and modern and the section Nancy had to enter was split by a long hallway that had to be shared by anyone moving from the interrogation room to the bathroom. Nancy recalled her vision of the murder and mentally cringed at the idea of squeezing past a killer in such close quarters.

Though she tried not to show it, she was relieved when Greg turned the knob on one of the half-dozen identical doors that flanked the corridor. Inside, Patterson, Hawkinson, and Mayer gave her quick smiles and brief nods of recognition but turned their eyes almost immediately back to the small black-and-white TV monitor. It sat in the middle of a long table that lined a wall at the end of the room. Above it, wires and cables poured down through a missing ceiling tile to stacks of electronic equipment. Patterson sat at the table with headphones on and the other detectives were perched behind the two desks in the room. If the lobby was tense, this room was a coiled spring. Everyone in it knew that prosecution of the Mary Allen murder hung on this final interrogation. If the suspect broke, the case would be closed. If he didn't, the suspect would walk.

Sacco seated Nancy in one of two empty chairs at the table and then took his own place beside her. He donned earphones and positioned himself comfortably in front of the amplifier, where large needles swung to the right as he told Carl that Nancy had arrived. On the monitor Carl waved in the fleeting, preoccupied manner of a man keeping his finger on many buttons. "Give her the mike, I want to see if I can hear her," he said.

Greg hit a button on its base and nodded to her.

"Hi, Carl," she said as she shifted around in the desk chair, trying to get comfortable, and plopped her bulky purse under the table.

"That's good. Just keep your volume up and don't fade on me. I want to know what this guy is thinking."

"How's it going so far?" she asked.

"We're just getting to know each other all over again."

"That must be a treat."

Carl's head jerked suddenly toward the door. He assumed a relaxed but commanding air for the benefit of the subject who was now returning.

Nancy's stomach tightened as her mind recalled the raging monster she had experienced at the Allen house. He had come into her mind as a terrifying figure whose machinelike knife thrusts into the elderly woman's body were fueled by a mindless rage that

had horrified Nancy even in her imagination. He seemed mon-
strous. Now he was only a few feet away.

She braced, but the figure that walked behind Carl and seated
himself at the interrogation table was so ordinary that for a
moment she wondered if she and Carl had been grossly miscom-
municating. His demeanor was tentative, his manner almost
apologetic.

"You're out of paper towels," the suspect said helpfully.

"My idea," Patterson said. "Thought it might annoy him."

"Sounds like he's happy for the chance to be helpful," Mayer
said.

"No," Nancy joined in. "He's annoyed. By being helpful he can
hide the irritation, but it's there, I can feel it."

But as she said it, doubts nagged at her. She was unnerved by the
discrepancy between the feel of the person on the monitor and her
visualization. Mental feel was normally foolproof. Physical man-
ifestations were much easier to mask. But this time it was the feel
that was wrong. His body seemed animated by a different soul
from the monster at the murder scene.

When Nancy returned her focus to the monitor, Carl was staring
down at the subject.

"So?" he said.

The suspect's aura flashed red again. But it was only the hue of
an average person irked by an obnoxious remark.

"I thought you'd want to know, that's all," he said. He seemed
surprised at Carl's response.

"Thanks. We'll take care of it," Carl said, a little frustrated at
the subject's control. He switched tacks and reopened the questioning with a line designed to provide some insight into the
suspect's thinking. "Where were we?"

The suspect shrugged.

Carl knew very well where they had left off. Nancy believed that
the mutilation of the victim could be traced to a hatred of women
stemming from the suspect's unhealthy relationship with his own
mother. He couldn't express this directly, so when a woman made

him angry, she inadvertently tapped into a volcano of rage.

"Your mother," Carl said. "I asked if you loved your mother."

"She's the greatest," the suspect replied, almost too quickly.

Nancy felt a mild version of a familiar feeling—anger.

"Anger," she said into the microphone. Greg looked at her a little puzzled. He had seen nothing angry about the subject's response.

"But do you love her?" Carl asked.

"My mother would do anything for me."

"That wasn't my question," Carl said.

"You know. She's my mother," the subject said with a friendly smile, as if the friendliness of his manner would pacify his increasingly frustrated questioner.

"Very angry," Nancy said. She felt for a moment like she was playing hide the eraser—warm, hot, hotter...

"Why won't you tell me if you love her?" Carl demanded.

Flashes of vivid color now danced in the suspect's aura. Yet his demeanor remained composed.

"This is upsetting him; he's getting really hot," she said into the mike.

"Sure you're not picking up Carl?" said Hawkinson. "He's the only one who looks hot to me."

Nancy had never seen anything like this in her life. The man on the monitor seemed to be earnestly trying to answer questions he didn't see the point of from a man who clearly thought him despicable. It was easy to feel sorry for him, even to become angry with Carl.

But psychically the picture was quite different. And the disparity was jarring. Never had she seen someone whose behavior was so detached from his inner life and whose inner life was so shielded. She wouldn't have thought it possible. It was not until Carl had raised the subject of the young man's mother that she recognized the man's feel and placed it at the Mary Allen house. She suddenly found herself worried about Carl's safety.

"Why won't you answer my question?" he demanded. "We all

have nice stories about our mothers, but that's not what I asked you. I asked you if you *loved* your mother and you won't answer."

"Look, Carl, I don't like the way this questioning is going. I'm answering your questions. I'm sorry if they aren't the answers you want to hear, but that's your problem."

The detectives in the room exchanged astounded looks. Suddenly the self-effacing, earnest young man was gone and a much more confident adult was talking to Carl.

"I'd say he just got through to something," said Nancy. But she worried that the suspect was close to walking.

"Back off," she said into the microphone, but Carl's instincts had already softened his approach. He paused to evaluate this new development.

"Okay," Carl said, sitting down across from the suspect. "Let's talk about something else. What do you do with yourself when you're not working?"

That seemed satisfactory. For the next fifteen minutes Carl listened as the suspect rambled on about his habits and his hobbies. When he mentioned shopping, Carl asked if he ever shopped at the Concord Mall.

"Sure," the suspect said. "All the time."

"Why there?" Carl asked.

"I like the stores," he said. "Especially..." He paused. When the sign came it was so fleeting that afterward they would wonder if they had only imagined it. Only because it had struck them all were they sure it had even happened—that and Nancy's assurance that the suspect had shifted briefly from his flat, shielded posture to an instant of deep satisfaction and pleasure. What the detectives had seen, or thought they had seen, was an evanescent smile pass the suspect's lips as he said the name of the store where the marshmallows had been bought.

Carl was dumbfounded. He had seen it too. He decided to throw what he had at him and see what happened.

"You know we found the murder weapon," Carl said.

"No," the suspect said, "I didn't."

"Actually, it was found shortly after the murder, but we just got confirmation from the medical examiner that it was the right knife."

"That should help," the suspect said.

"It was a steak knife from Acme," said Carl.

"Oh, I think I know exactly the kind you mean. My mother shops there and..."

In the room where Nancy sat, the detectives had gone suddenly rigid, halting even their breathing so as not to miss even the inflection of what came next. Inside, Carl too was frozen, but he knew it was critical to appear outwardly nonchalant. He scratched his neck as he looked with casual and polite interest at his suddenly garrulous subject.

Nancy knew but decided not to clutter Carl's racing mind with the fact that the suspect was not being tripped up, but was in fact very much in control. She could feel in him playfulness and confidence as clearly as she had felt his anger before and his rage at the murder scene.

"...Didn't they give away steak knives or something? In fact, I think that's how we got ours."

"Oh?" Carl said.

"Yeah, I think so. I know we got plates that way and some other stuff. My dad tells her not to get started, that you can save some money, but you always end up with an odd number of things because she can never remember to buy the things every week and then the promotion ends."

"And they're so common," the suspect was continuing. "That's the other reason my dad doesn't like them. He hates common things, says it's like drinking out of jelly jars."

He had smiled. This time Carl was sure. It was fragile and brief, but sandwiched between all that earnest naïveté it was a smile.

"Sonofabitch, he's laughing at us," Mayer exploded. The others looked at him. He had articulated the thought on all their minds.

"Take a look at this," Carl said, handing over a photograph of the teacups. "See anything unusual about this photo?" He dropped it on the table between them and watched as the suspect picked it up with his left hand and gazed at it dutifully.

"That's Mary's kitchen," he said after a moment. Carl nodded. The suspect looked back at the photo. "It wouldn't be like Mary to leave cups out like this. She'd wash them up and put them away. I don't think I ever saw anything on that counter."

"Was Mary right-handed or left-handed?"

The suspect thought for a moment. "You know, I'm not sure," he said.

"Right," Carl said, and allowed himself an instant of optimism. But warning bells were going off inside Nancy as she felt a familiar pattern building within the subject. It was only moments later, when Carl pointed out that the direction of the handle on the cup suggested that it had been used by a left-handed person, that the smile came again.

"Yes," he said in the manner of a fascinated student, "I can see that. But Carl, you don't think that just because I'm left-handed, I would have killed her?"

The interview went on for several hours after that, but it might just as well have ended then. Carl had never seen anything like it. He poked and probed, built carefully and painstakingly toward questions or disclosures that should have at least rattled the subject. But at the moment when a breakthrough seemed inevitable, the momentum would inexplicably dissipate and it was as if Carl were talking to a new subject.

On breaks, Carl would join the squad and ask for input. It was during one of these brief meetings that Nancy explained that she saw four different people in the suspect. There was the earnest young man, the confident adult, an almost wimpy child who was genuinely hurt that Carl could think him capable of something so despicable, and the personality Nancy had experienced at the murder scene.

"The problem is that when you work on one, before it becomes vulnerable, another one moves in and takes over," Nancy said. "I hate to say it, but the one that is most heavily shielded is the killer.

If you can get to it, he might lose his composure," she said. Her observation did little to lift spirits.

As the interrogation proceeded, Nancy tried to discern from the suspect's aura when Carl seemed to be poking in a spot that might get beneath the defending personalities. Occasionally the probing would begin to rattle the suspect's composure, but that only brought out the assertive young adult who would make it clear that much more of this badgering and he was walking.

In the end it was Carl who terminated the interview.

Nancy waited in the room while the detectives watched their prime suspect leave. As Carl walked with him to his car, he chatted casually, and as the suspect closed his door and rolled down his window, Carl leaned over and in his most sincere manner took one last shot.

"Just remember," Carl said. "The Delaware State Police have a long memory and we're always going to be here. There's no statute of limitations on murder."

The suspect smiled but said nothing.

As the detectives dragged back into the room, their disappointment was palpable. It was 2:30 A.M. Nobody could say they had not given it their best shot. But that thought was little comfort.

Carl was the last to enter. He looked over his tired, frustrated team and shook his head. "Sonofabitch enjoyed it."

To this day the Mary Allen murder remains an open case. No one has ever been charged.

Six

While Waiting

By the fall of 1976 Nancy was learning that disappointment and frustration were as much a part of police work as they were of becoming a mother. No leads had yet surfaced in the Jack White robbery, and even then it looked unlikely that the Mary Allen murder case would ever be closed. On the other hand, her pregnancy was progressing. Consistent though gentle nudging from her own mother, as well as some timely suggestions from Dr. Green, had begun to pierce Nancy's formidable defense system.

At her five-month checkup in August, Dr. Green had sat her down, peered across the desk in his best fatherly manner, and asked Nancy if she had yet prepared a room for the new baby.

"No," she said.

"Have you bought any baby clothes?"

She ducked her head slightly.

Doctor Green smiled. "I understand what you're thinking, but now I really think it's time you started to get ready to have this baby. It's doing fine."

He paused and Nancy looked up.

"You're not doing very well but the baby is fine. Now I want you to get ready to have this baby. I want you to go out and buy some baby clothes."

"No," Nancy said.

Dr. Green sat for a moment, patiently waiting for Nancy to think about what he had already said and trying to shape his thoughts in a way that might get through to her. Finally he smiled.

"Nancy, I understand you're afraid, but this baby is going to be born and it's not going to have anything to wear."

Even she had to smile at that. When she got home, she called her mother in Dover and told her what Doctor Green had said. Harriet Myer was tickled. Among her own tactics had been to mail Nancy baby blankets. By the end of the conversation they had set a date to visit an off-price retailer called Wilmington Dry Goods. The possibility of a child began to become more real to Nancy from that day forward. She realized too that she must begin to get the boys, at least Travis, ready for a sibling. Her own doubts were forced to the background as she took on the task of preparing the boys.

Other preparations were more tangible. She and John had gotten rid of the paraphernalia used for the boys as infants, a ritual that had helped steel Nancy against the hope of having her own child. Now she had to accumulate it all over again on a tight budget.

Harriet reminded her that the well-worn crib Nancy had used for the boys when visiting their grandmother was still in her attic. It was a solid wooden product that just needed a coat of paint. The idea of giving that lovely old relic new life with a paintbrush appealed to Nancy. She agreed instantly to redo it.

Not long after, Travis came home from school one hot day in early September to find his mother seemingly jailed inside the wooden bars of his old crib. The sight startled him and stirred worries about how she was ever going to get out.

It was Travis's nature to worry and the pregnancy had given him more than ample cause. Even Harriet had voiced concern over

Nancy's lack of color and stamina. John had taken over care of the boys pretty much completely, and though this suited Blake just fine, Travis didn't especially like having his father replace his mother on a day-to-day basis.

He would often sit down with his mother, pat her hand, and say, "It's going to be all right, Mom. The baby's going to come and then you'll feel better."

But his eyes made it clear that he wasn't telling as much as asking.

"I'm sure that's just what's going to happen, and then I'll feel a lot better. But I'll need you to help with your new little sister," she would say. "New babies are a lot of hard work."

"Mom," he protested, "you don't know it's going to be a girl."

"Yes, I do," Nancy said. "You know how Mom knows things. I've seen her eyes. She has beautiful blue eyes."

Travis clamped his mouth shut in a gesture of skepticism, but his eyes looked up at her in wonder and curiosity. He was a natural pragmatist, but secretly he believed his mother was truly magic.

Magic, but sometimes impractical.

The fact that she was penned in, painting the bars she would have to lift to get herself out, struck him immediately as a predicament.

"Mom," he said, "how did you get in there?"

In truth Nancy had approached the task methodically, measuring the crib height off the floor and her own exact dimensions from back to belly. It had been a close fit, but she had been able to inch under the frame until she could sit up through the mattress opening. She had then pulled the paint can under and stood. Close quarters, but doable.

Travis listened to her explanation doubtfully. After measuring with his eyes first her and then the crawl space, he shook his head.

"You know, Mom, you're in trouble. You're not going to be able to get out of there. Then what are we going to do with you?"

"It's okay, T-Bird, I figured it all out. I was very logical. Besides, I got in; why wouldn't I be able to get back out?"

"I don't think you can," he said after sizing up her belly and the crawl space once again.

Nancy switched tacks. "Well, if I get stuck, you guys will have to come in here and lift the crib up and get me out."

"No," said an increasingly agitated Travis, "I don't think we can do that because we might drop it on you and hurt the baby."

Finally Nancy tried to send him off to get her a glass of water, but he refused to go.

"Mom, you don't want to drink water, because then you'll have to go to the bathroom."

She shook her head and resolved to finish quickly so that she could relieve his worries. While working, she tried to keep Travis distracted with questions about school and stories about things that had happened to him in this very crib. When she finished, Nancy laid the brush across her open paint can and confidently turned to him.

"Okay," she announced confidently, "I got under here and now I'm going to get out the same way."

She squatted, then plopped down on her back. She eased her feet under the frame. Lying flat and inching across the floor, she quickly realized that she was in trouble. True, she had fit under the rail an hour before, but two things were now different. The baby had moved, raising the apex of her belly a good inch or so, and the bar was now wet with fresh paint. She couldn't brush it as she had getting in.

From across the mound of her belly, she could see Travis near tears.

"It's okay, T-Bird," she said as she wiggled and angled and dragged her body one way and then another.

"No, it's not," he wailed. "I told you and now you're stuck and I can't get you out."

Blake had gone immediately from school to play and John would not be home from work for several hours. The hopelessness of the situation was too much for Travis. He began to cry.

"It's not a problem, Travis. I'm fine in here and I have you to keep me company."

Travis looked up at her as though a new idea had suddenly crossed his mind. He ran into the kitchen and came back with a plate of cookies and a glass of milk and passed them dutifully into her. Not only could he take care of her, but he had Mom all to himself. He was now smiling.

"How about some music?" Nancy said as she munched her second cookie.

"Sure, Mom," Travis said. Again he was off, returning this time with his Fisher-Price record player and a book.

"Wanna read a story?" he asked.

Nancy sighed to herself. She might be stuck but the real crisis had been averted.

That was not the last time Nancy had to head off pregnancy-related trauma for her two adopted boys.

It was fall when Blake came bursting in, marched to his room, and slammed the door. Travis trailed behind and went immediately into his parents' bedroom, where he buried his face in his mom's pillow.

By the time Nancy got to the bedroom, Travis's complaint was a soggy mixture of sobbing and "I hate her, I hate her," muffled by the pillow into which the words were directed.

"T-Bird," she said, sitting on the edge of the bed and rubbing his heaving shoulders. "What's this all about?"

"I hate her, Mom, I hate her," he repeated.

"Hate who?" Nancy asked, though she pretty well knew.

"Julie. I hate her. She's mean."

"What did she say?" Nancy asked with a sigh.

Travis clutched the pillow into which he had been crying and brought it around with him to hide his face.

"That you're going to throw me and Blake in the trash," he said.

"You mean because we're going to have a baby?" Nancy said.

Travis buried his face in the pillow and wagged it up and down.

Nancy had been expecting trouble from Julie. She was an only child, a little older than Blake. Whenever her grandfather visited, he made a special point of playing with Blake or Travis, because he knew they didn't have a grandfather. Sooner or later Julie was bound to become jealous.

"Now why do you suppose Julie might have said that?" Nancy asked. The pillow moved from side to side.

A muffled "Because she hates us" came out of the pillow.

"Look, T-Bird," Nancy began, "you know there's a world of difference between kids that just happen and kids that are chosen, don't you?"

In the background she could hear Blake's door quietly opening, so she waited for him before continuing. As he climbed up on the bed, Nancy could see that his eyes were dry but a little bloodshot. He had a thumb in his mouth and his "baba" clutched to his chest. Baba was his stress management device. To most other people it looked like a pillow shaped like a panda bear. Between his thumb and his baba there wasn't much he couldn't handle. This afternoon, though, the panda bear's ear was tear-stained.

"I hate her, Mom," he said with focused rage.

"I hate her too," Travis said, letting his pillow slide down so she could see his face over the top edge.

"Listen, guys," Nancy continued. "I chose you and Blake. I didn't have to. When you adopt, they grill you with all these questions and make you come back time and time again and show you pictures and tell you all about the children and then you pick. And even after you pick, you still have to wait another day in case you change your mind. You really have to want a baby to adopt it. Now, do you think that after all that trouble we're going to just throw away something we want so much? This baby was a big surprise. It's going to be a pain in the neck for a while and then eventually it will be a nice person like you."

Nancy was making some progress, but she hadn't quite turned the corner with Blake. When Travis said he hated Julie, she worried about Travis. When Blake said it, she worried about Julie.

"Blake, remember what you said to Olga when she said she was going to fix it so I could have a baby?" Blake feigned faulty memory and shook his head. "I think your exact words were 'Neat, Mom.' You said how neat it would be if I had a baby. Now you can't go changing your mind just because Julie gets you mad. That's not fair to the baby."

Blake looked at his mother as if to ask how she remembered so much. But she did and she had him. Whatever the consequences, he had voted for a little sister.

"Mom's right, Trav," he said, patting his brother on the shoulder. "What's Julie know? Her parents didn't even pick her; she just happened."

Through the summer and into the fall, Nancy's relationship with the Williamses continued to grow. She found herself on the phone with Kitty almost daily. They talked kids mostly, but one day in September Carl came home while they were talking and Kitty excused herself to make him lunch. It suddenly struck Nancy that Carl always came home for lunch and she could never remember him eating at a restaurant.

"Oh, he won't," said Kitty. "He only eats at home."

As she thought about how inconvenient that must be for a detective, she became aware that Carl was about to be faced with a dilemma. "Well," she said to Kitty, "he'd better brace for something. He's going on a trip."

"Oh no," Kitty said matter-of-factly. "He doesn't travel. They know it and never send him on trips. He turns them down."

"He won't be able to turn this one down," Nancy replied.

"Carl, you're going on a trip. Nancy says," she heard Kitty say.

"I don't go on trips." He sounded uninterested.

"She says you're going on this one."

"Oh, yeah? Who's going to make me?"

"Smitty," Nancy said.

"Smitty," Kitty relayed to her husband.

There was a long pause as Carl chewed on Nancy's premonition. "I don't travel," he finally said.

Two days later Nancy was banging on the Williamses' front

door.

When Kitty opened it, Nancy greeted her with a wink. "Where's Carl?" she asked. Kitty pointed to the den and Nancy made a beeline down the stairs.

"Give me a map, give me a map," she ordered.

"A map of what?" Carl asked.

"The East Coast."

Carl, who was seated in his swivel rocker, looked at her with a frown. Kitty provided the map. They unfolded it in his lap.

"Here and here," Nancy said, pointing to two spots. One was Boston and the other was Quantico, Virginia.

"What's that?" Carl asked.

"That's where you're going."

"Not me," Carl said, sitting back. "I hate to travel. I mean I *hate* to travel."

And he had always been successful in talking his way out of travel by arguing caseload. He was too busy clearing cases to be going to schools or conferences.

Nancy just smiled.

It was two weeks later that Maj. Ray Deputy, head of operations for the Delaware State Police, called Carl at Troop 6 and broke the news.

"Guess what?" He sounded like a man about to do someone a big favor.

"What?" Carl asked.

"You're going to the FBI Academy."

"No, I'm not going to the FBI Academy," Carl said. "I don't travel."

"You're going to like this," Deputy said.

"What is it?"

"Homicide school. It's only two weeks."

"Ray, I don't have time. I'm clearing cases."

"This will be good for you. It will make you a better detective."

Carl didn't agree, but he found that after Nancy's premonition, he couldn't muster his usual zest for argument.

Deputy called back two days later even more effusive. "Oh boy, are you lucky," he said. "I got you into the most prestigious school we have."

"Give me a break," Carl pleaded. "Where now? No, don't tell me. Shall I tell you?" There was a puzzled silence on the other end. "Boston," Carl said.

"How did you know? You got a spy down here?"

"No," Carl sighed. "Not exactly."

What he actually had was a phenomenon and word was getting out. He didn't understand exactly what Nancy did, but he could no longer disbelieve it. The trips had nailed it for him.

She wasn't always letter perfect, but she was right often enough—and sometimes in stunning detail—to stand the hair up on the back of your neck. As word spread, Carl was cast in the unlikely role of booking agent as requests for Nancy's services grew.

Col. Irvin Smith was so pleased with the results of his recruitment of Nancy that he planned a special luncheon and award ceremony in her honor. His only dilemma was how to keep the certificate and another gift he had prepared a secret. She would have to know about the luncheon—he personally arranged the day with her for October 4—but once that was decided, he was careful not to contact her directly. He would have his secretary inquire about her availability for cases and referred detectives through Williams.

But his efforts were only partially successful. When the colonel called and said he wanted Nancy to come down and meet some of his majors, she knew instantly she would be receiving an award. The image of a certificate formed in her mind but there was something else that she didn't quite understand. Floating in front of the certificate was an image of Colonel Smith as a young man decked out in his state police uniform with the high boots and wide-brimmed hat of a trooper.

The day of the luncheon she was escorted into the colonel's office. Smitty was on the phone, but two other officers were there.

One was Maj. Ray Deputy, whom she had already met. Deputy's job was among the most stressful in the state police. As head of operations, he was responsible for the day-to-day deployment of over four hundred men. The tension had taken its toll; he had developed high blood pressure. Through Williams he had become aware of Nancy's work as a meditation teacher. One night Carl had taken her to Deputy's house to see if she could help. Nancy had taught him deep, regular breathing. Then with her low and gentle voice she had led him into the most profoundly relaxed state he had ever experienced.

"Surround your whole body with green moss and just relax," she had said. The techniques he had learned from her he used to handle stress throughout the rest of his career.

But today it was Nancy who was stressed. The pregnancy had made her self-conscious. Her maternity wardrobe was severely limited. She had opted for a plaid shirt with a white collar that she hoped would suit a luncheon with the top officers of the Delaware State Police. But no matter what she wore, she felt, well, big. Big and awkward.

Smitty waved and rose as he talked on the phone, and Major Deputy greeted her warmly. Smitty quickly hung up and came around in time to introduce the other officer—Ben Ewing, deputy colonel and second-in-command of the Delaware State Police.

Ewing was tall and thin; his build reminded Nancy of her own father. He had blond hair that was beginning to go gray and blue-gray eyes. Smitty called Ewing "gentle Ben," because of his easygoing nature. The one thing that was not easygoing about Ewing was his faith. As a devout Christian, he was having trouble with police use of this lady who could foretell the future.

Nancy had heard about this potential antagonist at headquarters, and meeting him did little to calm her already nervous stomach.

Smitty had wanted the pair to meet, convinced that once Ben met Nancy, his reservations would evaporate. But on this occasion he had brought Nancy down to thank her for her volunteer work and the last thing he wanted to see now was her put on a witness stand. Still, once he introduced her to Ben, his friend took matters into his own hands.

Nancy sensed that Ewing was reluctant even to shake hands with her, fearful that he might be embracing Satan.

"I'm Ben Ewing," he said and then it seemed to Nancy that in the same breath he asked, *Do you believe in God?* In truth he had merely smiled, said hello, and asked if she would mind if he inquired about a couple of things.

Nancy agreed, so they walked over to a corner of the colonel's office where they wouldn't be disturbed.

Smitty recalls that they were off for perhaps ten minutes and returned as best friends. While he had expected Ben to come around, even he was surprised at how quickly the transformation occurred.

Nancy didn't know what she was about to face, but now that she had met Ewing, found herself surprisingly composed. She had probed his motives and found he was a sincere and gentle man who simply wanted to know what he was dealing with.

"Do you believe in God?" he asked.

"I have a very strong belief in God," Nancy told him.

"What church do you belong to?"

"I am a baptized Methodist," she said.

That seemed to please him. He seemed to struggle with his next question but finally asked, "Do you think your information comes from God?"

It was a difficult and loaded question, but Nancy just answered with the same reasoning she had provided herself.

"I really don't know. I think it comes from the same place that all creativity comes from. Certainly our gifts intellectually come from God. But whether it's God directly speaking to me I don't know."

Nancy looked over at Smitty, who was trying to carry on a nonchalant conversation with Deputy; both men looked worried and restless and ready to come to Nancy's rescue if necessary. Ewing was getting down to the bottom line.

"Do you think it could be the devil?" he finally asked.

"No," Nancy answered unequivocally.

"What makes you think that?"

It was a question that she herself had raised during her opening. The answer that she had arrived at had come from considerable soul searching. "Because," Nancy began, "I think if it were the devil, the information wouldn't be accurate. It would be misleading and it would waste a lot of time. Nothing positive would come from it. It's been my experience that when you are dealing with evil, what you get is not productive. It is negative. It just plays games with people. And this ability has not been functioning in that way."

Ewing chewed on that for a while and then a big smile spread across his face. He extended his hand and patted Nancy's shoulders as they returned to the other two men.

Smitty immediately relaxed and Deputy, as if on cue, departed the room and returned with a large brown envelope. She opened it and saw the certificate of appreciation she had visualized.

"Did you know you were going to get that?" Smitty asked.

Nancy cringed, but had to admit that she had in fact seen it when Smitty first invited her to lunch.

She was surprised when Smitty didn't seem disappointed. "Go get that other package," he said to Deputy.

Ray again left the office and this time returned with a small box. This time Nancy was genuinely curious, but as soon as she touched the package, the image of Colonel Smith in a trooper's uniform appeared in her mind.

"What's this?" she asked.

"We did it," Smitty said. "We did it." He was clearly tickled and the two other men were grinning from ear to ear.

"Open it up," Smitty said.

She pulled open the flaps. Inside was a pewter statue of a Delaware state trooper in exactly the same position as her visualization of the colonel. When she explained this to the assembled officers, Smitty and Deputy looked at each other and shook their heads.

"The colonel modeled for that statue," Ray explained.

The luncheon was Nancy's last official contact with the police for more than a month. Knowing that she was eight months pregnant was one thing, but seeing her so far along had quelled any inclination Smith might have had to bring Nancy into cases until after the baby was born. The exception came November 9, when headquarters wanted to know if Nancy could help them with a thirteen-year-old autistic boy named Zandy Bisson who had wandered off the grounds of the Hospital for the Mentally Retarded near Stokely and had been missing for almost a week.

"A week?" Carl screamed into the phone. "You boys are right on top of this one."

There was silence on the other end.

"What do you want her to do?" he finally said.

"Find the kid."

"I'll ask," Carl said, then, thinking of his own four children, added, "Never mind. I know what she'll say. Get me some of the kid's possessions. You know, a stuffed animal or something. And a picture. Have the chopper put down in the parking lot of the Our Lady of Grace Church. That's about three blocks from her house. I'll get her there and you can fly her down with you."

He then got on the phone to Nancy. She was happy to help but reminded Carl that Heidi was due anytime.

"Maybe a good helicopter ride is just what the kid's waiting for," he said.

"That's okay with me," said Nancy, "but you might want to let the pilot know."

When Carl arrived at Nancy's, there had indeed been a change of plans. With him was a young trooper wearing a black flight suit and military-style boots. In his hands he carried a large envelope and under one arm was squeezed a teddy bear. On his belt was a walkie-talkie.

"Sorry, Nance," Carl said. "They didn't want to help that baby get born. Said there was no way they were flying with an overdue pregnant lady. We're going to tell this pilot where he is and he'll direct the other pilot."

The pilot accompanying Carl seemed embarrassed as they moved immediately to the kitchen table. There he handed her the envelope and the teddy bear. From the envelope she withdrew a map, a Xerox copy of a photograph, and a sweater. The minute she saw the sweater, a chill ran through her. It was a dark green V-neck and full of feelings. But what bothered Nancy was that Blake had one exactly like it.

"They said it was his favorite," Carl noted as he noticed Nancy staring at the sweater.

The teddy bear was a well-loved chocolate brown bear with a smashed nose. It too began to give her information. But when she gazed into the eyes of the child pictured on the grainy sheet of copy paper, the urgency drained from her and was replaced by emptiness.

She looked up at Carl and shook her head.

"I'm not surprised," said the detective. "He disappeared last Wednesday and they just now thought of asking you."

"Well, let's get him found," she said.

Nancy closed her eyes and clutched the bear. The feelings she got were intense—brilliance and affection, sharp and rich, love that filled her and almost brought tears to her eyes. And from these feelings an image began to weave itself before her.

The scene that formed was surprisingly tranquil. A stream in a forest. The ground was thick with yellow and crimson leaves. One floated gently on the clear stream as it followed the current between the towering trees along the banks. She allowed the leaf to carry her with it until along the bank she saw a snatch of blue and froze the vision. She backed up and focused on the unusual color. It was a hat, and under it, well hidden by the leaves, lay the peaceful face of Zandy Bisson.

But the picture didn't match what she knew about Zandy's stature. The pile of leaves before her couldn't possibly be hiding a boy five feet tall. But as she framed her puzzlement, the awareness came that Zandy had somehow sunk into the soft earth. With this thought came a change in the picture in her mind to show his head arched to one side on his outstretched arm.

"It's no wonder you haven't found him," she said. "He's hidden. All but a piece of his hat the size of a saucer. He's stuck in the mud up to his arms almost, and covered with leaves. You've been near him. Searchers have been very close but he would be easily missed."

"We need some orientation," said Carl. "Look around and see if there are any landmarks."

She returned to the scene and noticed that to the left of Zandy was a tree bent almost to the ground. Not too helpful. She scanned the scene from above the boy and looked down at the surrounding countryside.

He's at the edge of a woods, not in very far at all," she said. "He's along a stream. To the northwest is a large brick building— about a mile away. And if you draw a line from that building across the woods and into an open field where I see a pond and a couple of what look to me like abandoned chicken houses, he's right on that line. He's where the line and the creek intersect."

She borrowed a pen from Carl and sketched a map of what she had seen on the back of the brown envelope.

"Have you ever been to Stokely, ma'am?" the pilot asked.

Nancy shook her head.

"Sergeant Williams, I've been flying over that area for two weeks and she's described it to a T. I know exactly where she's talking about and I also know that Lieutenant Sylvester and a trooper were in that area the first day of the search but didn't find anything."

"He's awfully hard to see," Nancy said.

"Is he still alive?" asked the officer as he rose and retrieved the sweater and bear.

"No," she said. "It's been too cold. He died of exposure."

Delaware State Patrolman Paris Mitchell was not a man to show his feelings easily, but his wife knew that the disappearance of Zandy Bisson was eating at him nightly. He would toss and turn and finally give up trying to sleep about daybreak, downing a cup of coffee and puttering around the house until it was time to join the search. He and his wife had three children of their own, and it was partly imagining how he would feel if one of them were lost in the woods around Stokely that gnawed at him. Temperatures at night were bone-chilling, regularly dipping into the twenties, and he knew that every hour the child was lost cut deeply into his chances of surviving.

Paris had been recruited the first day Zandy disappeared because he had grown up near Stokely and knew the area. It helped too that his mother had worked there at the hospital all her life, so Paris was also comfortable around children with special needs. From day one he believed that the boy would have been drawn to the creek that ran behind the hospital between Dodd's Pond and Millsboro Pond. All kids were drawn to water, but he had been told this was especially true of Zandy. There was a particular spot along the creek that was not especially wide, but it was deep, and it was there that Paris had found other kids who had wandered away from the hospital. He and Lieutenant Sylvester had checked that area the first day but found nothing.

Day after day the hunt continued, and when the official search was called off at the end of the first week, Mitchell took the week of vacation he had coming and with a handful of other searchers and support from the state police continued on.

His strategy was to begin each day around 8 A.M. and work from the hospital toward the town of Millsboro, about five miles away. This path roughly followed the creek he felt certain Zandy would have been drawn to and took him from open fields into a thick forest. If the creek were followed far enough, it led to Millsboro Pond, where the forest opened onto a farm marked by two prominent chicken houses. Each day Paris would mark where he had quit and return the following day to pick up the search.

On the morning of November 9, Mitchell's wife had joined him and two other volunteers worked nearby. They had been searching for about an hour when Paris crossed the creek and began walking back upstream. His path took him back into woods at about the point where he had been on the first day, to the area he had originally thought Zandy might have been drawn to. He had walked only about a hundred yards when a small patch of blue cloth amid the yellow and red leaves caught his eye. His heart raced.

"Zandy?" he called, automatically stepping up his pace. "Zandy?"

As he darted through the woods, the swatch of blue became a ski cap and the outlines of a face began to emerge from among the matted leaves.

"Zandy?" he said gently as he arrived at the spot where the boy lay. But his voice trailed off. Before him was the lifeless body of Barry Alexander Bisson. He was buried almost up to his armpits in mud and sediment. His right arm was outstretched. Perhaps he had been reaching for the solid bank. His head lay sideways, cradled by his shoulder, as if he were sleeping.

Sadness filled Paris Mitchell. It was a sadness that he didn't want his wife to suffer. He turned and shouted back to her not to come any farther.

"Go back to the hospital and call the troops," he said. "Tell them we found Zandy."

Carl had dropped the pilot off at the helicopter and was heading back to Troop 6 when the thought occurred to him to monitor the transmission between the enthusiastic kid he had transported to Nancy's and the helicopter above Stokely. One of life's small pleasures for him had become watching other cops go through the same transformation Nancy had put him through.

He flipped on the walkie-talkie in time to hear her report being relayed south. What he heard next surprised him. Instead of the standard "roger" and "stand-by," what came over the airways was a rather flustered helicopter pilot trying to tell his colleagues not only that Zandy had already been found, but that the description that had just been relayed was so accurate that it had made the searchers' hair stand on end.

Nancy was surprised when she got the call from Carl so quickly.

"They found him," he said. "And you just scared the shit out of a lot of people."

Seven

Your Daughter Is Very Psychic

The vision was powerful and disturbing.

"The lights," Nancy said. "Pulsating lights that pop on and freeze the dancers. Otherwise it's black. Frightening. Unreal. Like a nightmare. In fact she's having trouble because it all seems familiar to her, as if she's experienced it before. But she can't be sure."

One of the officers who sat in Nancy's Scottfield living room had never worked with her before. He was Detective Everett Chapman. Chapman, a nine-year veteran detective who worked out of Penny Hill, north of Wilmington. When Susan Spahn, a twenty-year-old junior at West Chester State College, disappeared from a popular discotheque one Saturday night in early November, the investigation had fallen to him. Unlike most cases, which worked their way to Williams's special investigative unit over a period of a year, the Spahn case was only a few weeks old when Smith brought Nancy in.

121

Chapman seemed anything but convinced that a psychic could help, especially one who looked about ten months pregnant, but he obediently brought along the requisite photos, map, and in this case a recent sample of the victim's handwriting, which Nancy had requested. Handed first the photos, Nancy was immediately struck by how pretty Susie was. Long blond hair framed an oval face. Her features were fine, almost fragile. Nancy gazed at the picture for a moment, her mind moving beyond the tangible image in search of a thought pattern. She got none. Probe as she might, there was no emotion to connect with beyond her own sadness. Either Susan Spahn was blocking with an efficiency that suggested complete amnesia or, more likely, she was dead.

Nancy put the picture down and focused on the map, which had the location of the discotheque marked. Almost instantly the images came swimming into her mind. Sound shook her body; lights froze young people like statues in unearthly colors. The scene throbbed with the forced rhythm of disco music.

One of the statues was Susie.

Nancy's point of view rapidly shifted to Susie's partner.

"He's a white male about six feet tall. He has thick, dark, wavy hair. Sometimes he has a mustache, but he will probably change that now to throw off suspicion."

As she offered more detail, the officers exchanged looks. Nancy's description matched the man with whom witnesses said Susie had left the discotheque.

"She's happy," Nancy said. As Nancy registered this, the vision flipped again as if to correct her. She found herself transported to a parking lot where the same young man stood before Susie, screaming at her.

"He gestures angrily toward the car. Susie fires back. She seems oblivious to his superior size and mounting rage."

Nancy strained to hear the words but the sound was too garbled. It was like trying to listen to conversation underwater. Nancy tried to locate landmarks by shifting her view around the parking lot, but when she did the image began to fade. Rapidly she refocused on the couple, trying to hold the image as long as she could. She knew this vision was useless to the investigation unless she could provide some actual landmarks, and as this need formed itself again in her mind, the phrase "jack-in-the-box" occurred to her. As it did, a small fast-food restaurant appeared behind them at the edge of the image. Susie broke off the argument and started to march toward it, but the man grabbed her arm and yanked her back. The argument continued.

As Nancy was drawn into Susie's increasingly desperate plight, she suddenly became aware of why this all seemed familiar to Susie.

"She dreamed it," Nancy said to the detectives. The words, once uttered, shook her with frustration. *She had precognitive dreams! Vivid, detailed, and still she didn't get it, when her gift could have saved her life.*

She looked at the detectives seated around her. Chapman looked puzzled but Carl and Greg were just looking at Nancy, waiting for more information.

"Susie dreamed her death," she said. Seeing the doubt written on Chapman's face, she added, "She told her roommate."

Chapman was not convinced, but Carl glared at him and he wrote it down. He had talked to the roommate, Diane Hummell, but she hadn't mentioned the dreams. He would have to talk to her again.

"The dreams were quite literal and vivid," Nancy added. "And she was frightened enough by them to tell her roommate. They came to her several times."

In fact, it was the most clear-cut case of a precognitive warning that Nancy had yet experienced, yet she realized this insight too was of limited use to a police investigation. She looked back at the picture of Susie and the vision returned.

Susie was getting into the man's car, she seemed angry. "He drives out of the parking lot, makes a right, drives down a road, and it isn't too much farther when he turns right again. That takes him onto a much smaller two-lane road off the bigger highway that he's been on.

"Then he drives part way up that road and turns left into a lovers' lane type of area. It's a short dirt road. I don't know what it's for. Then he pulls over.

"He is smoking and offers her a cigarette. She declines. They're talking."

"What about?" Greg asked.

"I can't get it word for word, but the gist of it is that he feels she thinks she's better than him and he's telling her that she's not. He says something about what he's going to do to her, that he's going to, well, have sex with her and steal all her jewelry and then they'd see who was better than who."

"What's she do?" Greg asked.

"It's odd. She has one ring that she's focused on. She's frightened but defiant. She tells him he can't have this one ring because it's got sentimental value to her. Something like that. He responds by saying he'll have that ring if he has to cut her finger off to get it."

Nancy looked up from the picture to break the vision. The threat startled her. The detectives were staring at her. She looked back down and continued.

"He makes an advance to her physically and she finally blows."

"What kind of advance?" Carl asked.

"He grabs her breast." She screams at him and reaches for the door handle. He's enraged now. He grabs her arm, hard, pulls her back, and…"

Nancy looked up again for relief from the escalating violence. "He punches her. And then it's like, once he hits her, he can't stop. The punch throws her head back against the frame of the car."

Nancy looked back at the picture, but her head bobbed almost immediately back up. "Oh my God."

"What?" It was Greg Sacco.

"She's getting it. The dreams. She's making the connection and she's terrified."

"Go on," Carl urged her.

Nancy took a deep breath, steeled herself, and resumed.

"She's desperate, knows she's fighting for her life now, and makes it out of the car. He comes across the seat after her and pulls her down. They're on the ground just outside the car. She's fighting him. She knows she's fighting for her life, but it's futile. He's so much bigger and he's on top, holding her. She gets one hand free and scratches at his neck and face, but that just enrages him more. He's punching her repeatedly. His arm goes back and down, back and down, and suddenly there's a gun in his hand."

"Where did that come from?" Carl asked.

"I don't know. He just has it and he didn't move from her, so it must have been on him or near him. And he hits her face with it. Hard, again and again. She goes limp. Now he's got a piece of wire in his hands."

"What kind of wire?"

"Wire. Thin wire. Thin silver wire. He puts it around her neck. He's strangling her."

"She's unconscious and he's strangling her?" It was Greg.

"He's..." She struggled for a word. *"He's caught up in it? Hateful."*

"So what's he do now?" Carl asked.

"Now that it's done, he seems surprised that she's dead. It's kind of weird. The rage is out of him. He's drained. Now he's frightened. He tries to decide what to do. He puts the body back in the car..."

"The trunk?"

"The front seat. He props her up. He backs out of the road that he's on and continues in the same direction he had been heading when he turned into this little road. He goes up to the next road and turns right. There isn't any traffic around. He picks the body up, carries it into the woods and dumps it. Then he gets back into the car and hightails it out of there."

"How far into the woods?" It was Carl.

"It's hard to tell from the way this comes to me. Maybe a hundred yards. The body lands next to some big boulders with initials on them. It seems odd in the middle of a forest like this, but it's some kind of preserve. It isn't wild. Not completely. And this doesn't make

any sense at all, but there's a manicured lawn that abuts the woods. I get the word Brandywine."

She looked up from the picture of Susie to the silent detectives. Chapman didn't know what to think. He had no reason to believe that what he had just heard was anything more than a clever housewife's imagination at work. On the other hand, she had gotten the description right, but maybe she had read that in the newspaper.

Carl and Greg knew better, but they were momentarily silent, allowing the primary investigator to have the floor. When Chapman didn't say anything, Carl did. He had learned that sometimes when he asked Nancy for the moon, she delivered.

"Okay," he said. "How do we connect him to the murder?"

Into Nancy's mind came an image that she could not make sense of, so she reported it without interpretation.

"There are two pieces of evidence that will be found with the body that will tie him to the murder," she said. "They are about the size of a matchbook, white or cream-colored. Irregular shape. Bubbly surface, little bumps on it. Plastic maybe. They will be easily missed if you don't know to look for them. And if you miss them, you may not get him. They will tie him to the case in a way he can't get away from."

"Is there anything else there?" Greg asked.

"There's the wire. It has some blobs on it and some kind of numbers."

"What is it?" Carl pressed her.

"It's the wire he strangled her with."

"If it's at the scene, it won't do us any good. Wire is wire," Chapman pointed out.

"It's not just wire," said Nancy. "It looks funny. It has blobs on it and the blobs have numbers."

"You mean electrician's wire?" Greg asked.

"I don't know what electrician's wire is," said Nancy.

Before departing, Nancy drew them a map of the area where the body was located. She described it as hilly and rocky, which was unusual for Delaware. "*I hear motors in the distance. Small motors. There is a river nearby.*"

At the door she was suddenly struck with the awareness that despite the detail she had provided, searching for the body now would be futile.

"*You won't find her until the last of the first snow of the year is still on the ground,*" she said.

Coming out of the blue, the prediction struck everyone, including Nancy, as odd.

"Well, we've already had our first snow of this winter," Greg said, "so I guess that means we have a long wait."

"She said 'year,' not 'winter,'" Carl observed. "Maybe she means January."

Nancy shrugged. She could offer no further help. The enigmatic quality of the information she sometimes received was frustrating even to her. The officers departed, crunching through some lingering leaves that had blown across the walk. The day was brilliant and crisp. But the world Nancy had just visited was dark, and the sunshine could do little to lift the pall it had cast upon her mood. Fall made her think of school and school was where Susie Spahn should be this day, with her greatest worry mid-term tests and a date for homecoming weekend.

Leaves scraped across the walk. The sound sent a chill through her. Inside her the baby stirred, and she withdrew into the warmth and safety of the house.

Dr. Green first put Nancy's delivery date at November 28. In fact, Thanksgiving was celebrated on that date at Nancy's, with her aunt and uncle from Washington and her mother all sharing the secret hope that they would be on hand for the event. But Thanksgiving came and went with no sign of the baby's imminent arrival. Within days, however, the false alarms began—painful cramps, the awful uncertainty of whether this was the time, and the anxious rush to Wilmington General's maternity entrance.

At first they acted these trips out with hopeful excitement, but as the days wore on and the baby did not arrive, Nancy's skepticism returned and she became reluctant to make the trip and subject herself to the probing and measuring required to determine whether this was the real thing. On Christmas Day the family once again gathered at the couple's Scottfield bungalow, reasoning that if Thanksgiving had been a good bet, Christmas was nearly a sure thing. Nancy did not disappoint—not entirely. The contractions came...and went, with a sixth trip to Wilmington sandwiched in between. All the while Heidi remained happily ensconced in Nancy's womb.

Frustrated, Nancy told herself she wasn't going to the hospital again until a foot was sticking out. But even as she made the vow, it occurred to her that she had always considered seven her lucky number.

Two days later Nancy was clearing the lunch dishes when she was frozen with the most powerful contraction she had yet experienced. It was sudden and brief. And when it was over, her legs had turned to Jell-O. She eased herself into the nearest chair. Other, familiar contractions followed, but the initial one had been different, scary.

She waited anxiously to see what her body would do next, but it seemed content to resume the rhythm of contractions she had been experiencing for weeks. She assumed it was just another false alarm. She tried to read but was unable to concentrate.

Her mind relentlessly posed the question: *When will it happen and what will it be like?* Much to her surprise, this time she got an answer: *The seventh trip. It will be rough.*

Frightened by her new awareness, Nancy tried to push it out of her mind by concentrating on the book, but with no success. *In her imagination she saw the eyes. They had become familiar to her by now—two blue-gray eyes with a striking line of dark blue around the iris. They seemed to study her. She knew they were her daughter's eyes. They were reassuring to a degree, but the eyes also stirred within her concern about whether she would be able to bring her baby safely into the world.*

The seventh trip. It will be rough.

The words seemed to guarantee little, except that it would soon be over.

Putting down the book, she walked into the baby's room. The pale yellow crib with the deer on the end was made up with sheets the boys had picked out. Folded neatly on the side rail was the cross-stitch quilt Nancy had made for Blake. He was "lending" it to "his" baby. She ran her fingers lovingly over the Snow White and the Seven Dwarfs figures. Dopey was her favorite.

Her peace was shattered by another great contraction. She braced against the crib rail as the strength drained from her legs. Pain roared through her and with it came fear. How much could her body take? How much could the baby take? She tried desperately to use the breathing she had been taught, but the pain made thinking hard. And into that vacuum of thought swam an image of a round-faced, blond beauty of a baby girl.

Heidi?

Her answer was love, a tangible sense of affection and well-being that flooded her body and momentarily washed away the pain.

Nancy scrambled into the nearest chair, and when the contractions eased, lay down on her bed to rest. To rest and think about Heidi.

Travis came looking for her, as he often did when he sensed that she was upset. He climbed up beside her on the bed and chatted away about little things, all the while reading her face for signs of trouble.

"Mom?" he said. "It's coming, isn't it?"

"I think so, T-Bird, but I'm not sure."

"This is it. I know it, I just know it." He snuggled next to her and they comforted each other.

Blake burst into the room. Seeing his brother getting hugs, he rushed the bed, bounded onto it, and scrambled to his mother's other side. They made a Mom sandwich and Nancy suggested they get a game they could play on the bed. Blake ran off and came back with Candyland, his favorite.

Nancy dozed intermittently as the boys played.

By dinnertime, Nancy was unable to sleep but too weak to do much else. She lay in bed and tried to play solitaire. John fed the boys and restlessly paced back and forth between the living room and their bedroom. In the bedroom, he timed the contractions as he'd been taught to do in their classes.

"Four minutes apart. Don't you think we'd better call Dr. Green?"

"Not till there's a foot sticking out," Nancy said.

The boys watched TV until their bedtime, sneaking up the hall from time to time to wave at their mother.

"Doesn't she have to come before her bedtime, Mom?" Travis asked hopefully.

"Babies come when they're ready, T-Bird."

Pressing his nose to the side of her stomach, he said, "Hurry up in there," then collapsed in laughter at his own joke.

Long after the boys were asleep, John found Nancy struggling to keep the breathing going around nearly nonstop contractions. He ran for the phone.

Dr. Green ordered him to get her to the hospital by force if necessary. He explained to John that she might not be too sensible right now and he should just ignore that. If he couldn't get her to cooperate, call him back and he'd order an ambulance.

"I'm not going in an ambulance," Nancy yelled. "I'm going in our car."

Getting to the door was another matter. It seemed as though a contraction attacked her with every step. John and the wall braced her as she tried desperately to use the breathing to distract from the pain. Fear loomed large, but she fought it with the lovely image of the round-faced baby.

Arriving at the door of their car, Nancy discovered that she could no longer bend to sit down. John panicked, not knowing what to do. Luckily, their next-door neighbors, Al and Marty, rescued them. Marty sent John and Al off hunting pillows to change the contour of the seat, then she took over the Lamaze coaching and calmed Nancy down. The neighbors offered to stay with the boys until Nancy's mother could get there.

The car flew out of the driveway. Every bump set off more contractions. Nancy tried to maintain the breathing while John tried to get there fast without getting killed.

"I think maybe I waited too long," she said at one point.

"Understatement," John muttered as he navigated the streets around the hospital for the seventh time. At the emergency room entrance, he ran for a wheelchair. She watched through the doors as he gestured to an orderly, who sprang immediately into action, grabbing the nearest chair and racing out to the car.

The orderly opened the car door and knelt down beside Nancy. She was battling a contraction. He helped by talking her through it. When it eased, he edged her toward the wheelchair. Weakened by the force of the contraction, she couldn't help much.

"Don't worry, missy. You just sit there and let me do the work," he said.

A nurse who had helped Nancy on one of the previous trips joined the orderly. Another contraction raged through Nancy's body.

"Oho!" said the nurse. "Looks like this time you're going to have this baby."

As they lifted her into the chair and hurried into the hospital, the contraction eased.

"How many trips does this make?" the nurse asked as she wheeled Nancy into the examining room.

"Seven. My lucky number is seven," she managed to answer.

Dr. Green hurried in and measured the strength of the contraction by the tightness of her stomach muscles. He listened for the baby's heartbeat and smiled reassuringly. "She's doing fine."

Nancy's mind wandered aimlessly, filling with inconsequential trivia. *Funny how even Dr. Green had called her a her all along.*

Dr. Green stripped off his gloves and talked her through the inevitable onslaught of contractions he knew would follow his pelvic examination. "This is your lucky trip; you're finally having this baby. It's gone too far for her to back out now."

As the evening wore on and Nancy became more and more tired, she realized the true significance of the term *labor*. This was the hardest work she'd ever done in her life. The contractions had grown so severe that at each one's peak, she neared unconsciousness. It was at one of these peaks that they detected a change in the baby's heartbeat. Nancy was rushed into delivery.

A spinal anesthetic was administered and she was warned not to raise her head. "You won't feel a thing next time," said Dr. Green.

So when the next contraction hit, she was caught off guard. It was the worst yet. She screamed in agony. Nancy tried desperately to focus on her breathing as stunned nurses jumped in to help.

"Why didn't you tell me you were in that much pain?" Dr. Green asked in the brief respite.

"How would I know, I never did this before," Nancy gasped.

Finally in the distance she heard voices urging her to look at her baby girl. Struggling to remain conscious, she looked down. Slowly, a baby swam into focus. He lay in Dr. Green's gloved hands. *So lovely, so perfect. Why are they telling me it's a girl?*

"It's a boy," she crowed.

Dr. Green peered around the little head, puzzled by her reaction. Then he let the umbilical cord drop away.

"It *is* a girl, look at her, a real baby." Nancy could not believe this was real.

"What did you think you had in there, a watermelon?" teased Dr. Green. As he turned back to the baby, he realized Nancy was silent.

She was gazing at the infant. Fear closed around her throat. *Shouldn't she be crying?* Dr. Green suctioned mucus out of the baby's throat. A bellow instantly split the awed quiet of the delivery room.

"She's alive, she's alive, she's really alive," Nancy screamed as Dr. Green held up the squealing ball of life for Nancy's amazed examination. How odd to know that she had grown a whole baby in her belly. A shadow passed over her mind, a touch of fear wandered through; something was still not right but she was too tired to pursue it further.

In recovery, nurse after nurse came in to congratulate Nancy, partly because they had heard about her history of miscarriages and partly because Heidi was the first baby girl in the maternity ward after an unusually long streak of boys. They all commented on how beautiful she was, but no one appreciated her beauty more than her mother, who was content just to lie there watching her breathe. Heidi seemed equally content watching her mother. She lay, eyes wide open, examining everything. The nurses and Dr. Green told Nancy this was not typical of newborns. Usually they are so tired they go right off to sleep.

By the time they were moved to a room, Heidi had fallen asleep. Nancy felt on guard somehow. She lay in bed watching her baby through the nursery window. Every now and then Heidi raised her head in protest and cried out, her face contorted with pain. Again and again Nancy tried to get the nurses to respond to this cry. They smiled and told her she just had the new mother jitters.

As the night wore on, weariness spread through Nancy, yet she felt somehow more alert. She was sure something was wrong and the knowledge kept her on edge, out of reach of the sleep she so desperately needed. The nurses tried to help her sleep by drawing the curtain so she couldn't watch the baby, but Nancy insisted they open it.

Oddly enough, the new mother in the room with Nancy sensed something was wrong too. Together they watched Heidi as she periodically raised her head and seemed in pain. Nancy started keeping track of the episodes on a napkin. By dawn they had grown more frequent.

Nursing her that morning was wonderful. Whatever was wrong, it wasn't interfering with Heidi's appetite. She was a healthy eater. It tickled Nancy that as she nursed, the infant twirled one foot round and round.

"I'll bet that's the foot you've been kicking the slats out of me with," she said to her. To Nancy's surprise, Heidi stopped nursing and seemed to smile.

When she had finished nursing, Heidi was put down to sleep, but more episodes of the pained expression and crying kept her awake.

It was noon when they discovered why Heidi was crying. As Nancy nursed her, Heidi suddenly went lifeless. Nancy watched in horror as the baby's toes started to turn black and the discoloration traveled quickly up her body. Then the left side of her body started jerking. Nancy hit the nurses' buzzer, but no one came. She turned the baby over, fearing that she was choking to death, and smacked her smartly between the shoulder blades. A shuddering breath passed through Heidi. Nancy turned her over and Heidi gazed back at her through a huge smile. Yet it was clear something was quite seriously wrong. Nancy struggled to the door and screamed down the hall, "My baby has stopped breathing."

Nurses ran from all directions. Heidi was plucked from her mother's arms and placed in a bassinet as question after question was fired at Nancy. But even as she tried to answer their questions, her eyes were glued on Heidi. Horror struck her as she saw Heidi's tiny foot turn black.

"She's doing it again," Nancy screamed.

All eyes turned to the baby as a nurse scooped up the bassinet and ran into the nursery, hitting buttons on the wall as she went. Despite efforts to get her breathing, Heidi turned blacker and blacker. Medical equipment and doctors with their white coats flapping flew by Nancy's room and into the nursery, where they worked on Heidi. Tears streamed down Nancy's face as she watched her child nearly die, time after time. Finally the baby was breathing again.

Nancy's roommate had gone home that morning. Alone in the room, she sobbed, "I told them something was wrong but they wouldn't listen." Then quietly into her knotted fists she prayed like she had never prayed before. "Please, God, let me keep this one, please let me keep this one."

Heidi was placed in an Isolette and wheeled out and down the hall. No one told Nancy where they were taking her. She got up and instinctively followed. A doctor who was questioning the nurse about what had happened caught the movement out of the corner of his eye and hurried in to talk with Nancy.

"Your daughter is having some kind of seizures. We're taking her to intensive care. Now tell me exactly what you saw. The nurses say you knew something was wrong. What cued you?"

Carefully Nancy described the episodes she had witnessed during the night and told how they had increased in frequency and intensity. Nancy handed him the napkin on which she had written the time of each episode. It was easy to see they had been getting closer all night.

The doctor hurried off. Nancy sat alone in the room staring in shock at the window where Heidi had been. Suddenly she felt a huge scream of fear in her mind and realized that Heidi, separated from her for the first time, was reacting psychically. Reaching out with her mind she touched the infant, assuring her that Mom was still nearby. Heidi's answer came in calmness.

The doctors discovered that the newborn was bleeding on the surface of the brain from the forceps delivery. The bleeding was stopped. Fortunately, the doctors were sure there was no permanent damage to the brain itself. The crisis had passed.

Encouraged to visit Heidi often, Nancy wandered down at all kinds of odd hours. No matter when Nancy came, she found Heidi surrounded by nurses working on her. Not only was this frightening to the worn-out new mother, but it was frustrating as well because they were able to hold Heidi and she was not. On one visit she burst into tears.

"I just want to hold her. Can I please hold her?" she pleaded.

The nurses helped her slip her arms in the portholes and placed Heidi carefully into Nancy's hands. Heidi smiled instantly, but alarms went off all over the place.

"Never mind that, her heart just speeded up," said a nurse. "Come over here and look at Heidi," she called to the other nurses.

"She's got that smile on her face again." They all watched her intently, then they looked at Nancy.

"It's her mom!" They laughed but did not explain what they were talking about. Nancy stood until she nearly passed out, content to hold her smiling, sleeping beauty.

The next morning one of the young pediatric neurologists took Nancy aside.

"I think there is something you should know about your daughter," he said. Nancy felt the fear rising up in her again. She braced. "Some parents might be upset about this and I don't know if I should tell you, but it's something I feel you need to know. Your daughter is very psychic."

Nancy stared at the doctor in amazement and then burst out laughing. Hurt, the young doctor blustered around, trying to explain what he meant. Nancy laughed even harder.

"Please. I'm not laughing at what you're telling me. I already know that. I thought you were going to tell me something awful. I'm elated to hear it's something normal like this. I'd be surprised if she wasn't. You see, I am a professional psychic myself. But how did you figure it out?"

"She kept setting off the alarms. Her heart rate would increase and she had this slaphappy smile on her face every time. We log in everything on the baby's chart. We noticed that three minutes after she would do that, you would show up to visit. There was no pattern to your visits. Yesterday it happened again when you picked her up, the same dopey smile and increase in heart rate. She knows when you're coming!"

Out of curiosity the nurses and Nancy compared notes and found out that Heidi was picking her mother up about the time Nancy hit the elevator button on the third floor. It took three minutes from that point for her to enter the intensive care unit. Nancy was relieved. That also explained why the nurses were always with her when Nancy came down to see her. They were responding to the alarms.

Her seizures under control, Heidi came home one week after

she was born. John was administering a final and couldn't get away so she was escorted home by members of Carl's unit in a Delaware State Police car that the detectives had decorated with pink crepe paper. Carl Williams drove.

Eight

The Big Payoff

*H*eidi's seizures never returned. In fact, the newest Anderson seemed robust in her curiosity and anything but fragile in her willingness to explore and test to get answers. Two early habits particularly fascinated Nancy and John.

As a birth gift, one of John's great-aunts made Heidi a crocheted ball. It was about five inches in diameter and consisted of red, white, and blue patches sewn around stockings. From day one it had been a favorite of Heidi's. She held it, slept with it, and pounded on it, but it was not until Nancy taught her to roll it that anything peculiar happened.

Heidi was in her crib and Nancy was on the phone the first time she noticed it. Nancy was looking out the window but, as always, was monitoring Heidi out of the corner of her eye when she thought she noticed something odd. The ball, which Heidi had pushed away from her toward the opposite side of the crib, appeared to move determinedly in that direction for a short distance, then roll back. At first the reversal startled Nancy, but she quickly reasoned that the crib mattress must have a slight incline.

She excused herself from her call and walked into the living room, where she could get a better view. Heidi, who usually greeted her with a huge grin and some baby gibberish, remained transfixed on the ball, which she was just sending out again as Nancy neared. It moved out about twenty inches, drew to a stop, seemed to quiver ever so slightly, and then returned to Heidi at an accelerating clip. Nancy studied the crib, looking for a slope, but could find none.

Heidi grabbed the ball as it slammed back into her and sent it rolling back out. Again it got no more than twenty inches when it slowed, seemed to quiver, and then returned to Heidi, who was now giggling and wiggling with glee at her game.

"Let's try this out here on the carpet," Nancy said as she slipped her hands under Heidi's armpits and lifted her out of the crib. She plopped her down on the living room rug.

Before lifting the ball out, however, she could not resist giving it a little push along the same patch Heidi had been sending it. It skittered easily off and did not stop until it bumped into the bars of the crib.

Too hard, Nancy said to herself, though she knew better.

She lifted the ball out and put it down in front of Heidi, then stood behind her and waited. Heidi turned and looked up at her mother with a huge smile.

"Ball," Nancy said. "Make the ball come back."

As if she understood, Heidi turned back to her ball and pushed it away. She glared at it and cocked her head to one side. The ball reached its limit, quivered slightly, and then came rolling back. The dog, who was curled up on the sofa watching this experiment, was suddenly airborne. He surrounded the ball and howled at it.

Subsequent attempts by the boys, Nancy, and John to duplicate Heidi's feat were unsuccessful. Try as they might to think it back, the ball just kept rolling, no matter how softly they pushed it out.

Nancy thought about the earnest resident in Wilmington and

how surprised he would be to find that Heidi was not only psychic but telekinetic—she had the ability to physically affect things with her mind. Telekinesis was one of the few areas of psychic functioning in which Nancy did not seem to be especially gifted.

Just having Heidi was magic, but to find she had inherited these special abilities was a bonus. Nancy wondered if her own father, seeing Nancy share his rapport with animals, had entertained the idea that their mutual gifts might go further. She suspected that he thought about such things secretly but, because of the time in which he lived, said little. He was too curious and open-minded a man to have ignored them. Publicly, however, while her parents had never discouraged her belief in things psychic, they had not especially encouraged it either. With Heidi it would be different. Nancy would help her take her gifts as far as she was comfortable.

The other peculiar thing they noticed about Heidi was the way she would bravely explore anything within the living room area rug but never venture onto the cold wood floor. The boys tried teasing her off the rug by placing toys just beyond her reach, but no matter what toy they used to coax her, she would scramble to the rug's edge but not beyond.

It was not until Nancy attended a lecture by Olga Worrall that she discovered that Heidi's reluctance to go beyond the rug's edge had a simple explanation. Heidi's eyes were badly crossed, impairing her vision. She was navigating by her sense of touch and felt safer with the familiar rug beneath her.

As Nancy approached after Olga's speech, the healer immediately recognized her and smiled at the blanket-cloaked infant held against her chest. But Olga's smile quickly gave way to concern as she gazed into Heidi's eyes.

"The turn in Heidi's eyes is more than that typical of an infant," Olga said. Then she looked Nancy squarely in the face. Her voice was stern, instructive. "She will need surgery as soon as it is safe. The surgery will be successful and it will not need to be redone if you follow the doctor's recommendation."

Nancy did not fully understand the last part of Olga's instructions, but she left the lecture hall grateful for her advice. She was also frightened and a little depressed by the prediction. Even if the surgery turned out all right, she felt Heidi had had enough medical problems and deserved an easier infancy.

Nancy raised the issue with Dr. Katzman at Heidi's next checkup. The pediatrician looked closely at the eyes but said it was too early to tell. He suspected the baby might have a problem because the turn-in was so extreme, but he deferred making a determination until her four-month checkup. When Nancy returned in April, it was clear the problem was getting steadily worse. A large portion of both irises were lost behind the infant's nose. He referred Nancy to Dr. Gordon Bussard, an ophthalmologist and eye surgeon in Wilmington.

Dr. Bussard was a towering man—six foot four at least, with a healthy shank of black hair and a gentle manner. Nancy explained Heidi's condition and behavior to him. He moved around in front of Heidi and withdrew from his pocket two tongue depressors. One had a sticker with an image of a panda bear on it and the other Raggedy Ann. He offered them to Heidi and asked her to pick the one she liked.

She immediately gurgled and grabbed Raggedy Ann.

Doctor Bussard smiled and tried gently to extricate the depressor from Heidi's grip. She wouldn't let go. His smile became slightly uneasy as he pulled harder and finally got his tongue depressor free. Again he moved it back and forth in front of her. But instead of tracking the stick, she glared at the doctor. Then tears started pouring down her cheeks, but no sound came out of her.

Dr. Bussard shook his head and smiled. "This happens sometimes," he said. He then handed Heidi the Raggedy Ann and produced another one.

When the examination was over, Dr. Bussard said an operation could correct the eyes. He would go in through the eye socket and adjust the muscles to pull her eyes back to center. The procedure had a very good success rate, but it was not without risk.

Then he made an unusual request. "Usually we do this in two operations, because as the child grows, the muscles change. But I think with Heidi we can do it once. I'll just have to overcompensate the correction. The risk of that is overcorrecting, which would require a second operation."

Recalling Olga's prediction, Nancy nodded her consent. The operation was set for August.

On the strength of her growing reputation, that spring found two important police organizations inviting Nancy to address their annual conferences. It was at the International Association for Identification, Chesapeake Bay Division, in May that she found herself making one of the strangest predictions of her career.

The meeting was held at a hotel in Dover, where Nancy presented a psychic version of hide the eraser. The audience was divided into small groups. The groups took turns leaving the room while Nancy hid objects. Those not searching were told to visualize the objects where they lay, and the searchers were told to tune into these images as they attempted to find the objects. The exercise demonstrated to officers that their intuition could be a valuable tool in police work. Nancy had discovered that the find rate was always nearly 100 percent and the officers were invariably surprised at discovering their own "psychic" talents.

After her presentation, Nancy was invited to the banquet that evening and to cocktails in the group's hospitality suite. Although she didn't drink and choked on the cigarette smoke that always accompanied these functions, she enjoyed talking to cops and quickly accepted.

The suite itself was jammed with people. As Nancy had feared, a cloud of smoke hung low from the ceiling. She had just entered the room when Sgt. John D. Heverin, of the Delaware State Bureau of Identification, the man who had arranged for her talk, came bursting through the crowd. He dragged Nancy over to an FBI agent.

"Nancy," he said, "I'd like you to meet Paul Bell. He's with the

FBI out of Dover."

Nancy, sensing that something was afoot, smiled warily and Bell nodded in return. He struck Nancy as easygoing and accessible, and it occurred to her how useful this would be in his work. When they shook hands, an image of him at home surrounded by his family filled her mind.

"Paul has a question for you, Nancy," said Heverin.

"Oh?" Nancy said.

"I thought if you could predict what my next interesting case is going to be, well, if you can do that, then I'll have a lot more confidence in this, uh..." The FBI agent groped for the right word. Nancy decided not to help him and he eventually let the sentence tail off. Starting again, he said, "What will you need to figure that out?"

"Well, if I can really do this, uh...," she imitated the agent's loss for words, "I shouldn't need to know anything, should I?"

Everybody laughed and Bell let his mirth settle into a challenging grin.

In truth, Nancy worried that she would not be able to work in the crowded, smoke-filled room. It was teeming with powerful impressions and loud voices. But as more and more people got wind of the test going on across the room, the noise began to subside. Nancy touched the agent's mind with her own and was immediately confronted with a vivid and horrific image.

From the hotel suite she was transported to a rural setting under a brilliant and cloudless sky. In a grassy area that appeared to be a courtyard of some sort she saw piles of dead and rotting corpses.

This can't be, *she thought to herself.*

Somewhere in the world she had left and to which she instantly wanted to return, she heard the words, "Oh, you don't have to do this," and she wondered to herself if on some unconscious level agent Bell too had knowledge of his next interesting assignment.

Nancy answered, "It's a multiple homicide and it's pretty brutal and it's one person."

Nancy didn't want to go into any more detail, but someone in the growing crowd of listeners urged her on with questions. "Multiple homicide? What are we talking about? Two? Three bodies?"

Nancy brought herself back into the room. "There are hundreds of bodies," she said.

Bell was incredulous. In a voice louder than he intended, he repeated Nancy's words, "Hundreds of bodies?"

Nancy now became aware that the room around them had grown still and everyone was glued on her. "All at once?" Bell continued.

"Yes," Nancy said. "They died in very close time to each other."

"What was the cause of death?"

"Asphyxiation."

"How many perpetrators?"

The scene swam back into her mind, and this time a single face rose out of the middle of a pile of bodies. He was an average-looking white male in his thirties. He had dark hair, but what frightened Nancy were his eyes. In them she saw madness. The visage kept growing until it eclipsed the scene beneath it and filled her mind. A chill went through her. Nancy brought herself forcefully back into the room and looked at Bell.

"One," she said.

"How could hundreds of people be strangled at the same time by one person?" Bell asked. "One person could not asphyxiate hundreds of people and not have one get away, get help, and get it stopped."

"Look," Nancy acknowledged, "it's so irrational, I think it must be wrong. But this is what I'm seeing. *Piles of bodies under a midday sun. Some picnic tables and all these dead people. There are children in the piles. It's awful. That's all I see. And silence. It's utterly quiet. Not even a breeze.*"

She looked around the room at the officers, who hung silently on her words. Suddenly she felt very exposed.

"This just doesn't make any sense," she said. "I don't know how anybody could asphyxiate all these people. This is crazy. I gotta be wrong. It has to be wrong."

The room seemed to relax at Nancy's recanting, but when the conversations had resumed, Bell looked at her and said, "You watch. I'm going to get stuck with that mess."

Paul Bell called Nancy more than a year and a half later. At first he didn't identify himself, but when he said, "Never let me ask you what my next interesting assignment is going to be," she immediately recognized his voice.

It was November 1978 and Bell was calling from a special hangar at Dover Air Force Base. Days before, a cult leader by the name of Jim Jones had ordered his followers to drink cyanide-laced Kool-Aid in the largest mass suicide in history. Although the cult had moved to South America, most of its members were United States citizens and the government had been charged with bringing their bodies home. A special morgue at the Dover facility, originally used for processing Vietnam War victims, had been set up to receive the victims of Jonestown.

Nancy, like almost everyone else in America, had read about the so-called Jonestown massacre and the fatal drink. When television news shows aired shots of the Jonestown compound, she had instantly recognized the scene. But it was not until Bell's call that she learned he had been assigned to help identify the bodies.

"You know how cyanide kills, don't you, Nancy?" Bell asked.

She did not.

"It paralyzes the breathing muscles," he said. "The victims are asphyxiated."

Within weeks of her presentation to the IAI, Nancy again found herself standing in front of detectives, this time at the Brandywine Sheraton north of Wilmington. Her audience consisted of homicide investigators from all over the world who were in Delaware to attend the Francis G. Lee homicide seminar, sponsored by Harvard University and the University of Maryland. Part of the purpose of the Harvard Associates in Police Science or HAPS, as the investigators' prestigious organization was called, was to provide police with the latest developments in laboratory and other scientific aids in crime detection.

The day of her speech was clear, cloudless, and stinking hot. Nancy had bought a new suit for the occasion, but by the time she had driven the un-air-conditioned Ford from Newark to the Sheraton, the outfit was wrinkled and she felt damp and disheveled. She was hardly in a good frame of mind to face what she thought might be her toughest and most cynical audience.

Gazing out over more than two hundred stern, stony-faced officers, Nancy began her talk by describing Colonel Smith's "polite police harassment" recruiting techniques, which brought a ripple of laugher. She relaxed a little. She then reviewed her cases, pointing out techniques that had worked and those that had not. Citing both flops and successes, she acknowledged the limitations of a psychic informant, but pointed out that when it worked, it was like having a unique eyewitness—but one that they probably would not want testifying in court. That too brought smiles. By the time she broke from her talk to demonstrate psychometry, the group seemed at ease and interested.

That changed when she asked for volunteers. Officers who had been even leaning forward in their seats suddenly straightened up and looked from side to side to avoid eye contact with her. Not a single hand went up.

"Oh, really brave cops we have here today," Nancy said, laughing.

"Here," said an officer to Nancy's right. "My partner volunteers."

The room broke into laughter and pretty soon officers all over the room were volunteering somebody else.

"Nope," Nancy said. "You've got to volunteer yourself."

"I'll volunteer," said an older man near the front. The volunteer was Martin M. "Matt" Puncke, a recently retired major from the Maryland State Police. Cheers broke out across the room.

Nancy looked at the man, who reached across the people seated in front of him to hand Nancy a black onyx ring with a diamond in the center.

Looking at some men seated in the general direction of her volunteer, she asked if they knew him and would judge the accuracy of her reading. They nodded.

Nancy closed her hand around the heavy ring and almost instantly feelings of warmth and generosity filled her body. She refocused on the audience and began with the words, "Sensitive and caring.

"This ring belongs to a man who would help people in need even if it was risky to him. The word *humanitarian* comes to mind."

Nods from her judges, and it seemed some blushing from her subject, though in the harsh glare of the lights it was hard to be sure.

"These are qualities that anyone who knows him would recognize, but he never flaunts them and prefers to help in the background. He doesn't do it for the visibility, but because it's needed and he asks nothing in return. He is close to his family; they are very important to him," Nancy said. She paused, then added, "Second only to his job."

Again, approving nods and laughter.

"But for all your humanitarian views, I wouldn't want to be on the other end of an investigation you were conducting, because you're so dogged. You're absolutely dogged. You just don't quit."

Then, looking squarely at her subject, she suddenly became aware that he was about to receive a significant award.

"Your humanitarian work will soon be rewarded with a gift," she said.

Almost immediately a man near her subject became very agitated. He looked hard at her, trying to get her attention. Although Nancy noticed his glare, she was so focused on her subject that she dismissed it.

"In fact, you're going to get that gift soon," she went on. "I would say..."

At that, the man behind Puncke was out of his seat and waving

Nancy off as if she were a jet trying to land on a sinking aircraft carrier. The gesture was so dramatic and unexpected, it stopped her in mid-sentence. She didn't know what to say. The Matt Puncke channel had suddenly been broken.

Luckily, the gesture was so sweeping that Puncke turned to see what the commotion was, which gave Nancy time to pray for some new piece of information. "A project that you have been working on for some time is nearing completion and will be quite successful," she concluded.

Puncke smiled as he walked up to Nancy, who handed him back his ring. He thanked her and then, loud enough for the audience to hear, said, "You really are quite good."

Applause spread throughout the audience as Puncke turned around and announced, "Okay, chickens, who's going next?"

Later in the afternoon, after Nancy had completed her presentation, she was asked to step to the front. The host thanked Nancy for her presentation and said they had a gift for her.

"But there's a catch," he added.

"Oh?" she replied.

"We want you to guess what it is."

With that, he handed her a rectangular package. Nancy immediately got the word *plate,* and before she could check herself, the word bubbled out and into the microphone.

Applause erupted even as she tried to correct her apparently erroneous reading.

"Well, that's pretty stupid," she said. "It can't be a plate, it's not even round."

The applause melted into laughter. She blushed with the embarrassment of someone who has said something funny but doesn't know what. It took only seconds to find out. The package contained a special decorative Delaware State Police license plate featuring her initials and the state seal.

It was a plate usually reserved for state legislators and high-ranking police officials. It filled Nancy with a sense of deep satisfaction. The message was, *You're one of us.* It overwhelmed her.

Pushing back a rush of emotion, she said, "See how logic can mess you up?"

The speech had gone well. So well in fact that a dubious detective from the Metropolitan Police Department of Washington, D. C., was on the brink of buying into Nancy's unusual abilities. His name was Otis Fickling, Jr. , and he was a rising star among homicide detectives. During eight years he and his partner Ronald Ervin had had a 97 percent closure rate and a 94 percent conviction rate. He was a feisty, suspicious man whose skepticism had been obvious during her presentation. Only after the demonstrations had he begun to shift, grudgingly. At the moment he was teetering but not sold.

As Nancy made her exit, Fickling and a group of his friends confronted her. The detective held a newspaper in his hands and had a determined look on his face. Yet he hung back.

"Go ahead, Otis, ask her," said one of the men near him.

"What was it you wanted to ask me?" Nancy said.

The story came not from Fickling but piece by piece emerged from the men around him as they told Nancy how HAPS was sponsoring a race that night at the Brandywine racetrack. A large contingent of members were going to the track that night and, well, they wondered if Nancy might, well, you know…

"Predict a race?" Nancy said.

"It was Otis's idea," said one of the men.

"He thinks you might be pretty good now because of the way you knew things about all those people. He wants to bet on the HAPS race."

"I don't want to make a prediction if somebody is going to go out and bet money on it," Nancy said. "If he lost it, I'd feel awful."

"I'd go out and bet it anyway and probably lose," Fickling said, finally pushing his way to the front of the group. "At least I might have a better chance if you told me who to bet on."

Though she knew instantly that what he said was true, it was not his argument that she found persuasive. It was the challenge, and her own curiosity.

Against a nagging sense that she was making a terrible mistake, Nancy asked if they had a list of the horses that would be running in the race. Before she could think about reconsidering, Otis pushed his already folded newspaper into her hands and pointed out the HAPS race.

Nancy gazed at the tiny agate type, not knowing what to expect. To her amazement the name Au Claire Fury suddenly turned bold and increased in size. Pointing to it, she said, "This is the horse that is going to win this race."

Fickling looked at the paper with a scowl but didn't say anything.

"You think I'm wrong," Nancy said.

"Oh yeah, I know you're wrong."

"Why do you think I'm wrong?"

Otis ran his finger down the horses and stopped at number seven. "This is the hands-down favorite and it's going to run away with this race," Otis said.

Nancy looked at the name and into her mind came an image of a horse tethered in a stable with several men tending it. They were examining its right rear leg.

"Ordinarily, you'd be right. Except that horse isn't going to run tonight," Nancy said.

Fickling looked at her with disbelief.

"It's got an injured leg. It's slightly injured and they won't be able to risk it. The horse is too valuable."

Nancy felt Fickling was still not buying it. *Covering her butt* was the thought she picked up from his mind. What he said was, "Well, if that horse doesn't run, then this horse has a much better shot than Au Claire." He pointed to another name.

"Oh, no. That horse is going to have a terrible night," Nancy said. She was surprised at the assurance in her own voice.

As she gazed at the tiny names, the number-one horse turned bold, just as Au Claire had. She told the others it would finish second. She had no reaction to any other name.

Fickling was anything but impressed and made little effort to hide it. Nancy was rescued by some of the meeting's organizers, who asked if she could attend their banquet the following evening. Nancy's mind raced. Politically, she knew she should attend. But what if she were wrong about the race?

In the end, she could think of little to say except that if she could find a baby-sitter, she'd love to attend.

When she got to the Ford, she collapsed. It had been a wonderful afternoon, but exhausting. Because they are trained not to let you know what they are thinking, police officers are tough subjects. Now her reputation was riding on her performance. Why then did she have to make that race prediction? After all her good work, the thing that would be remembered would be that race. If she were wrong...

She didn't want to think about it. Reminding herself that she always went into a slump after the adrenaline rush of a performance, she sighed and started the engine. *If I'm wrong, I'll be darned if I'm going to that banquet*, she told herself. But even as she thought it, she knew that hiding was not her style. She'd go, one way or the other.

Time dragged that evening, though Nancy's mother did agree to go with her to pick out a dress for the banquet. Nancy had nothing appropriate for so formal an affair. But there was little to distract her through the endless night. She tossed and turned, sleeplessly imagining being trampled by horses or jailed for false horse picking. She finally gave up and moved into the living room, where she picked up the latest *Reader's Digest* Condensed Book and read, eventually dozing off. She was awakened by fingers of the morning sun poking through the living room drapes. It was not long before the morning paper came flying onto the lawn.

Nancy hurried down the walk, grabbed it up, and for the first time in her life ignored the front page in search of the sports section. She flipped to the race results and ran her finger down to the seventh race. The name that had loomed so large to her the day before again jumped out at her: Au Claire Fury. It was the first name; it had won the race. She looked at the payoff: eighteen dollars. It had gone off a relative long shot. She quickly looked for the race favorite that she had predicted would scratch, but it was nowhere to be found. The other horse she had picked finished second and the show spot was a dead heat.

She relaxed for the first time since the previous afternoon. Suddenly she was looking forward to the banquet.

The ballroom at the Brandywine Sheraton was gradually filling with people as Nancy and John arrived. Most were filtering in from a small bar outside the room where a cocktail hour was still going on.

No sooner had the pair entered than a Delaware State Police officer with whom Nancy had worked cornered her and handed her an appointment book.

"This is from all your friends, Nancy. It's your schedule for the summer," he said.

Puzzled, Nancy opened it to find every weekend filled with names of officers with whom she had worked and the notation: "Brandywine Racetrack."

She looked up a little tentatively to find the room suddenly silent and looking in her direction.

"Of course, the split is open to negotiation," said the officer. Laughter and applause followed.

Nancy was flustered.

"I'd start right now by having a heart-to-heart with that Washington detective," someone said. "I hear he did pretty well for himself on last night's race."

"Where *is* Mr. Fickling?" Nancy asked in a way that suggested they'd better find out.

"Bermuda," someone shouted.

When the laughter subsided, one of the officers signaled in the direction of the ballroom and said he thought he had seen Otis and his wife already go in. Nancy nodded and she and John made their way to the receiving line.

At its end stood Irvin Smith, resplendent in his dress uniform and full regalia, a chest full of medals. He was beaming.

"I hear you did some good work yesterday," he said.

"I don't know if you can say picking a horse race is good work, but I guess I got it right," she said.

"I guess you did," said the colonel. "You know, I had those guys calling me from the guard shack at the track after the seventh, trying to get me to put them in touch with you so you could pick more races for them."

Nancy shook her head. "Thanks for not calling."

They laughed. She was as pleased for Colonel Smith as she was for herself. He had taken a lot of teasing from colleagues in other states about his belief in her abilities; she took special satisfaction in not letting him down.

"Over here, over here," she heard coming from one of the tables in the large room. She looked up to see Otis Fickling waving frantically in her direction. "Over here, Nancy. We saved you a seat. You have to come over and sit by me; we've been saving you a seat."

It seemed impossible that this was the same doubting Otis she had met little more than twenty-four hours before. The tables were beginning to fill up, so Nancy and John moved into the room and toward Otis.

"Come on, Nancy, I've been saving these seats all night," Otis shouted across to her.

She and John made their way to his table.

Otis introduced his wife and then started jabbering on about the night at the track.

"You know," Nancy said, "the paper didn't mention the favorite. Did she scratch like I said?"

Otis shook his head and laughed in amazement.

"Not only did she scratch, a bunch of us went down to the stable when they made the announcement to see why."

"Right rear leg?" Nancy asked.

Otis nodded.

"And that's when you decided to bet big."

Otis nodded again.

Nancy shook her head.

"How big?"

Otis and his friends at the table exchanged self-satisfied looks.

Two weeks after the conference closed, Nancy understood why Matt Puncke's friend had grown so agitated toward the end of her reading. The mail that day brought a letter from Matt. In part it read:

I left Wednesday afternoon because I had agreed to be a guest at the Laurel Rotary Club meeting at 6 P.M. The meeting had no special importance to me other than I had been invited by a friend. During the meeting, the President of our local bank and chairman of an award committee selected me to receive their national "Four Way Test Award." The committee had been working on the selection process for the past two weeks. I had no knowledge of the award or the committee's activities.

The award included a large silver wine cooler, fourteen inches high, all properly engraved. I had to relate your statement of a special gift made at 3 P.M. to the presentation and gift received at 7:30 P.M. I thought you might be interested in the immediate evaluation of your work.

Sincerely,
Martin M. Puncke
Major—Retired
Maryland State Police

Nine

1002 Shallcross Avenue

In February, a year after the assault, Carl's unit made an arrest in the beating of Jack White. It came when the unit cracked a five-man gang working out of Middletown. In addition to the assault on the young high school student, members of the group were found to be responsible for several murders, armed robberies, burglaries, and weapons thefts.

Their attacks were characteristically brutal. In one instance, a driver was shot to death at a red light when he tried to flee his attackers. During a robbery in Smyrna, a man's wife watched as he was fatally shot twice in the chest when he tried to resist the robbers.

Nancy's original reading had described three assailants, two of whom were later identified by Sacco as friends of Jack's from school. The pair had visited him at the service station shortly before the assault. The third suspect she had described was never sketched because of her error on the first two. But except for his race, which she had said was white, her description of a large, muscular man with a mashed nose generally matched that of Leonard Jenkins.

Jenkins, thirty, then an employee of Delaware Power and Light, was charged with the assault, largely on information provided by Clifford D. Johnson, another gang member who testified during Jenkins's trial that Jenkins came to his home the night of the White beating and showed him coins in bloodstained wrappers. Reports of the trial in the Wilmington newspaper quoted Johnson as saying that Jenkins had told him he had taken money from a young gas station attendant and that he had "choked him, pistol-whipped him, and kicked him." The testimony coincided with Nancy's reexperience of the assault at the Gulf station, during which she had felt metal crashing into her face. Perhaps most interesting, the section of Wilmington she had pinpointed on the map turned out to be near Jenkins's residence.

Jenkins was found guilty of first-degree assault, first-degree robbery, and two charges of possession of a deadly weapon during commission of a felony. At his sentencing in November of 1977 Jenkins was lectured by an angry Superior Court judge, who told him that what he had done to Jack White might be worse than murder and that Jenkins was remorseless and dangerous. He then sentenced him to three consecutive thirty-year terms.

While cracking the Middletown gang and obtaining a conviction in the arson case gave Carl's special investigations unit a boost, the disappearance of Susie Spahn haunted them throughout 1977. Nancy's original reading in the early winter of 1976 had predicted Susie's body would be found while "the last of the first snow of the year is still on the ground." Carl thought she meant early in 1977, but Greg thought she meant the following winter. Nancy later clarified her prediction—it would be January 1978—but for Williams that was too long to wait. The first snow of the new year found him and his men swarming over sites that coincided with Nancy's reading. When that first snow of 1977 melted and no body was found, they didn't give up.

It had not taken Nancy long to figure out that Carl Williams was a great detective partly because of his empathy for victims. It was the juice that fueled his intensity. The senseless beating of Jack White had been one of the most disturbing cases of his career. The disappearance of the college coed with the close-knit family nagged at him in the same way.

Not infrequently, Greg, Kitty, or Carl would call Nancy at the house with a hunch about a location that seemed to match her reading. Whenever possible, she would rearrange her schedule to accompany them. But often they would check in with her, then go off themselves looking for a wooded area in or near a wildlife preserve, somehow associated with the word *Brandywine.* Nancy had said that abutting the woods was a neatly manicured lawn. She had also seen large rocks with graffiti on them near the partially buried body. The sounds of small motors could be heard in the distance.

One evening in early spring Nancy stopped by the Williamses' house on her way home from a meeting in Wilmington to find Greg, Carl, and Kitty stunned by what seemed to be her synchronous arrival. They were convinced her popping in just as they were debating calling her was significant. Nancy protested that she was at the Williamses' two or three times a week, but the group was convinced that her arrival added credence to their latest theory on the location of Susie's body.

They had concluded that the portion of her visualization referring to snow meant that Susie's body had been hidden at a state depot for snow equipment. Nancy knew instantly that that was not what she had meant, but Carl wanted to check it out.

"What I said was that she's not going to be found until early next year," Nancy protested.

"Well, what if you're wrong? You've been wrong," said Carl.

"I know. But I know what my mind meant when I said that," she replied. "You just don't want to accept the fact that it's going to take a long time for Susie's remains to surface."

"Humor us," Carl said. Nancy had to laugh as they piled into his car and headed north toward Wilmington. The results of the foray to the depot were predictable, but Nancy didn't mind. She was learning that methodically turning over stones, however unlikely they seemed, was part of police work. Often, the logic of a hunch only became clear in hindsight.

On another occasion, Greg and Carl decided that maybe Nancy's reference to snow referred to the street name for heroin, so they took her to a section of Wilmington known for its brisk drug trade. That too proved to be a cold trail.

More than once, Greg met Nancy at the discotheque where Susie had last been seen and the pair spent the day attempting to retrace her route the night of her disappearance. The resulting course took them down Route 202, which fronted the Beaver Valley Shopping Center where the disco was located, and onto a narrow country road that ran between grassy fields and occasional patches of heavy forest. The road itself was a narrow, winding macadam snake.

Once they left the highway, Nancy was surprised at how quickly the dense commercial development melted into long stretches of desolate countryside. The road dipped and turned so often that a car traveling it at night could easily turn off into the woods without being seen. Aging stone fences in disrepair popped into view and then ended abruptly. During the day the grassy fields, herds of grazing cows, and occasional horse farms seemed safe and reassuring. But she could easily imagine how at night the same countryside could be desolate and terrifying.

After about ten minutes, Greg pulled the car into the Thompson Bridge area of Brandywine State Park.

The name, the terrain, the general location, and the proximity to the discotheque seemed to him to make it a likely location for the body. Nancy agreed. The two walked through the park for hours, searching for the rock with the initials Nancy had seen in her vision. But when the cold air and damp fields finally forced them to give up, they had found nothing.

During one of these searches Nancy turned to Greg and repeated her early warning, "When you find her, you will find something that will specifically link your suspect to her. It will be a crucial link. It's important that you make sure they look very carefully."

Det. Everett Chapman, the principal investigator on the Spahn case, had his own theory about what had happened to Susie. At least he had a prime suspect. From witnesses, Wysock had drawn a composite of the man with whom Susie had left the discotheque. When it was published in the newspaper, a reader called police to say she believed the man they were looking for was twenty-four-year-old David A. Dutton of Middletown.

Carl knew Dutton well. Not only had he personally locked him up on several occasions, but once when Dutton was arrested in New York and had to be brought back to face charges in Delaware, Williams got the job of transporting him. The four hours they spent together had convinced him that Dutton was a strange and dangerous man. In Williams's opinion he was cold and calculating, and he could kill in a heartbeat. Chapman too was convinced Dutton was their man. In their initial questioning, his story did not match that of Amy Barnes, the friend with whom Susie had gone to the disco the night of her disappearance. And Dutton had refused to take a lie detector test.

As a further test, Carl put together a photo lineup and ran it by Nancy. She too identified Dutton as the person whose thought pattern most closely resembled that of Susie's murderer. But without a body, there was little more they could do. At least with a murder charge.

However, that was not to say that they could not take steps to ensure that Dutton would be around if and when a body was found. When officers visited him in July as part of their ongoing investigation, they found a potted marijuana plant. This gave them enough probable cause for a search warrant. The search turned up a bayonet, machete, gun, and several other items that had been stolen in a Kennedyville, Maryland, burglary. Dutton later pleaded guilty to the burglary but denied that the gun was part of the loot. The gun was a .22 caliber revolver with a missing hammer spring and grips.

As the investigation into the Spahn disappearance continued, an odd thing occurred that shook Nancy's confidence in her reading. It was summer when one of the squad members called and told her a cousin had seen Susie at Wilmington Dry Goods, a popular clothing store. The cousin was especially close to Susie and felt absolutely certain she had seen her at the store.

"I hope it *is* her," Nancy said. "I hope for some strange reason she just walked away and started a new life." The minute the words were uttered, a voice inside her screamed, *No, she's dead.*

"But," she quickly added, "I don't think it's her."

"How do you explain the fact that her cousin recognized her?" the officer asked.

"Why didn't the cousin walk up and say hello?" Nancy replied.

"She tried but Susie was at a distance. They hailed her but she just kept going, and by the time they got through the crowd, she was gone. They lost her."

"Well, I hope it's her, but I don't think so," Nancy said.

It was not long before Nancy found herself having a similar conversation with Susie's mother. They had spoken before, and Nancy had soon realized that Mrs. Spahn was the kind of secondary victim who makes cops go the extra mile. She was sweet, cooperative, and patient with the tedium and redundancy of the investigation. Her pain was palpable, but she endured, doing everything she could to help whenever asked. Early in the investigation Carl told Nancy that Mrs. Spahn had asked to speak with her. Would she mind?

No, Nancy said, of course not, though she knew it would be a difficult assignment.

Mrs. Spahn made it as easy as she could, but at first it was awkward. They chatted about the weather; she thanked Nancy for working on the investigation. From that she eased into asking Nancy what had happened to her daughter. Nancy had no intention of rerunning the detailed tape she had played from her mind for police. Instead, she said simply that she believed Susie had left that night with a man whom she had no reason to believe was violent but who later became enraged and had struck and killed her.

Even such a brief summary was an awful thing to tell a mother. Mrs. Spahn asked specifics, but Nancy kept her answers as general as possible.

"A part of me thinks she's dead too," the mother finally said. "But a part of me doesn't think so." The comment took Nancy back to a picnic table on the Delaware River almost exactly a year before. She was sitting across from the father of Lee Cilimburg, trying to help him wrestle with the same conflict. She now felt the same responsibility to try and help this woman brace for the fact that she was never going to see her daughter again.

Finally Nancy said, "Susie was a very beautiful girl, and I have to tell you that I think that is true of her spirit as well. One of the first things I checked out was whether she would disappear, whether she was capable of inflicting that kind of pain on her parents, and it was clear she was not."

"I know," her mother said. "I've asked myself that question a thousand times and I don't think so either."

"I feel your relationship with her was particularly good, and even if she was fleeing from something, which I don't think she was, she would find a way to let you and her father know."

Mrs. Spahn started to cry and it was not long before tears were welling up in Nancy's eyes as well.

"I told the police that, but I'm not sure they believed me," she said.

"They believe you now," Nancy said. "Because they've said the same thing to me."

But with the sighting, everyone reconsidered. Her own doubts grew when within a week of the first report, one of Susie's teachers from West Chester called police with a similar story. He too had seen Susie at Wilmington Dry Goods and had tried unsuccessfully to hail her.

Police questioned the teacher closely. It turned out Susie had sat in the front of his class. He had a clear recollection of what she looked like. Two credible witnesses; two independent sightings.

Armed with pictures of Susie, Carl and Greg visited the retailer and flashed the pictures to employees. Sure enough, several said they recognized her as a recent customer. Carl had the store staked out, but as suddenly as the sightings had begun, they stopped.

Mrs. Spahn did not call Nancy very often, but the sightings stirred a deep and troubling conflict in her. There was the desire to believe that Susie might somehow still be alive. But there was also the sure knowledge that if Susie were in fact alive, she would not allow her parents to suffer in this way. To Nancy, Mrs. Spahn's struggle was evident in her voice. She believed that Mrs. Spahn herself was an unusually intuitive person and that the close relationship she enjoyed with her daughter meant that on some level she too knew that Susie had been dead since the night of her disappearance. But the mother's heart would not commit to that belief.

"I just keep hoping that your impression is wrong," said Mrs. Spahn. "That somehow..."

"I hope it is too," Nancy would say to her. "But I keep coming back to the fact that Susie wouldn't do this to you. If that's her, I can't imagine she wouldn't get a message to you that she was okay."

During a call that occurred after the last sighting, Mrs. Spahn finally said, "I can't imagine that either. She must be dead." And then she started crying.

When the sightings suddenly and inexplicably stopped, even some cops began to wonder if they had been some metaphysical phenomenon. Nancy believed they had a much more mundane explanation. While Susie was attractive, she was not that unusual-looking and she wore her hair long and straight—a popular style at the time. Because she was blond, her hair would dominate an observer's impression. Nancy believed the sightings were simply of a blonde who resembled Susie.

Wilmington detective Leroy Landon was a six-foot black man who, like Carl Williams, was consumed by police work. Unlike Williams, who had a wife and family to pry him away from the job from time to time, Landon had only the life of a bachelor to distract him. While Williams was obsessed with his cases, Landon lived them.

He was gifted with a quick wit, easy patter, and an unerring instinct for people. Landon dressed nattily, a handkerchief carefully folded in his breast pocket and one of his stylish assortment of hats covering his bald head. A carefully trimmed mustache framed an ingenuous smile that was so ingratiating it put even the most wicked suspect mistakenly at ease.

This dapper image was in sharp contrast with his persona on the street, where he was known as a dangerous man whom you didn't cross, but a man who could be trusted. It was a reputation that gave him unequaled access to sources, especially in Wilmington's black community.

In the late spring and early summer of 1977, Landon was one of more than a dozen detectives working feverishly to solve a series of rapes that had terrorized a well-to-do section of West Wilmington. In most instances, the women were accosted in their homes during daylight hours.

The first known assault occurred May 17 when a man broke into the victim's basement, confronted her with a hatchet as she was beginning to do her laundry, and threatened to split her head open. He forced her to undress, bound her hands with rope, and tied a bra over her eyes before leading her upstairs, where he raped her. Before leaving, her attacker stole money, jewelry, and the family's .25 caliber semiautomatic pistol.

A month later the same type of gun was used by a rapist who threatened another woman in a parking garage not far from the original attack. The woman was forced to strip, her eyes were covered with her bra, and she was raped in the backseat of her car.

On June 29 a man wearing a bandanna and wielding a gun

entered another residence in West Wilmington and raped its owner. Again the victim's hands were tied and her eyes were covered with a bra.

A fourth rape occurred on June 30 when a man came to the victim's door and asked to use her phone book. After looking up his number, instead of dialing it, he pulled out a pistol and raped her.

Although Nancy had not worked with the local Wilmington police, word of her success with the state police had quickly moved through Delaware's law enforcement grapevine. Pressure to find the West Wilmington rapist was intense, so Carl was not surprised to get a call from a detective in Wilmington.

Nancy had never worked a rape before, but she reasoned that she ought to be able to pick something up from the victims if she could meet with them.

It was night when they paid a visit to their first victim. Leroy drove and his partner, Jay Ingraham, filled Nancy in on the case. They pulled to a stop on a quiet residential street lined with towering maple trees that seemed artificial in the cold glow of the street lights. Leroy twisted in his seat and laid down the ground rules.

"We don't want this lady to have to relive the attack," he said. "So we won't stay long and we won't be asking her about what happened or anything. Can you work your," he wrinkled up his forehead playfully, "rez a rez without a lot of talking?"

Nancy smiled. " 'Rez a rez'?"

"Like abracadabra," Jay interpreted. "Magic?"

"If it's going to work, it shouldn't take any talking," she said. "How did you explain my coming along to her?"

The two detectives exchanged looks.

"We didn't exactly tell her you *were* coming," Leroy finally said.

"Too much press already without headlines about a psychic being brought in. Right?" Nancy said.

Again the detectives exchanged frustrated looks.

"Something like that," Jay acknowledged as they climbed out of the car.

"I won't volunteer it, but if she asks, I'm not going to lie," Nancy said.

When the door opened and the victim appeared, she was in semishadow. Nancy looked beyond her momentarily to what seemed a tastefully decorated home. Peach walls glowed with warmth. As Nancy stepped in, their hostess moved into the light and Nancy found herself startled by how closely they resembled each other. The woman was younger and a little shorter than Nancy but not much. Her long black hair was wound up in a bun and capped a long, angular face with brown eyes. *Sisters*, Nancy thought. At a distance they could be mistaken for twins. The realization that followed chilled her. She herself was the type of woman being stalked by the rapist.

Embarrassed by her own stare, Nancy began babbling about friends who had said they thought they had seen her in parts of Wilmington where she was quite sure she had not been. They laughed and the woman confessed to similar experiences.

As they proceeded down the hallway, Nancy was struck by the works of art that filled the townhouse. Indian baskets made of colorful coils of straw were displayed on the wall. In the sitting room Nancy's attention was drawn immediately to a sculpted child's head that sat on a small table. She knew immediately that their hostess had sculpted it and marveled at her talent.

Jay too was struck by the piece and asked if she had done it. The woman nodded. They chatted about the bust briefly, and then Leroy apologized for bothering her again but said that's how police work is. You just have to go over and over events, hoping to turn up a missed detail that might crack the case.

The victim listened politely, but it seemed to Nancy she knew somehow that this was not a routine rehash of the crime— especially since Jay and Leroy did not ask for any more details but instead just chatted. Nancy participated little in the small talk, concentrating on ranging the victim in an attempt to retrieve memories of the attack and attacker.

Suddenly the woman looked up at Nancy and in a polite but firm tone said, "You're not a policewoman, are you?"

"No," Nancy said. "I'm a psychic."

A relieved look spread across the woman's face. "I knew that name. I think some of my friends have been to see you."

Jay and Leroy sat helplessly as the two women talked animatedly about Nancy's work. When they were ready to leave, the woman thanked Nancy for trying to help and grasped her hand. It was contact Nancy had hoped for but was not planning to push. The physical link with the woman, deepened by their rapport, brought a flood of new images and feelings. *Suddenly feelings of terror and humiliation filled Nancy's body as images of the rape flooded her mind.*

"Are you all right?"

Nancy blinked and once again was standing on the stoop of the neat townhouse in West Wilmington. Her new friend was looking closely at her with worry in her eyes. It was nearly 10 P.M. and the sky was ink black. Trees blocked the lamps that dotted the street, leaving the women standing in the harsh glare of the house's light.

"Yes," she said. "I'm fine." Her voice was filled with new empathy for the victim. She squeezed the woman's right hand in both of hers. "We really have to find this man," she said.

Back in the car, Nancy was enthusiastic about new information she had picked up. The sketch of the assailant was close, she said, but the eyes were wrong. She could work with an artist to fix that. But the image she was now getting of the rapist showed him in a uniform of some kind. None of the victims had mentioned a uniform.

"It's like denim or something, white socks and black shoes. And above his pocket is a marking of some kind," she explained.

Jay pulled out his notepad.

"Like an insignia?" Leroy asked hopefully.

"I can't make it out, but it seems painted on, not sewn, pinned, or embroidered. It's ink. I think it has some numbers to it."

"Is it a patch?" Jay asked.

"No."

"What kind of insignia is it?" Leroy asked. "Military?"

"It's not really an insignia," Nancy said. "It's just some markings above his pocket."

Leroy looked at Jay and shrugged.

"Tell me more about the uniform," Jay said to Nancy. "What's it made of?"

"It looks like those work outfits you buy at Sears," she said. "That kind of cotton stuff, only with a shiny surface. It's blue. Short-sleeved. And the trousers look a little short."

"A hat or cap of any kind?" Jay asked.

"I don't see a hat."

"What about a car? What kind of car does he drive?"

"He always seems to be walking," Nancy said. "I don't see him in a car."

"Then he must live near the victims," Leroy said.

"Maybe he takes a bus," Jay said.

And then out of the blue Nancy added, "He's taking courses at a college. Some kind of classes."

The trio sat in silence contemplating a college student who dressed in a blue denim uniform with trousers short enough to reveal white socks with black shoes. That kind of student would stand out.

But what if he was a part-time student and the uniform was his work attire?

"He does have a job," she said. "He does some kind of maintenance."

During the next several days Jay and Leroy divided their time between taking Nancy to visit other victims and hauling her around to every institution in Wilmington where workers wore uniforms. They visited movie theaters, restaurants, gas stations, the post office, and finally Wilmington General Hospital, where Jay and Leroy paraded every type of worker from orderly to janitor before Nancy.

"Does it look like this?" Leroy would ask.

"No."

"Well, what's different? Does it look anything like this?" he would say, grabbing someone else from the hall.

None of the uniforms matched her vision. Finally, in frustration as she shook her head at a hospital kitchen worker, Leroy glared at Nancy and wagged an imposing finger in her direction.

"Lady," he said, "if you don't see that uniform soon, you're going to need this hospital." He said it with frightening intensity, and it was only when they saw the smile emerge from his mustache that they all relaxed and started laughing.

The other tack the Wilmington detectives pursued with Nancy was to use her as a human bloodhound. It had been her idea. Immediately upon leaving the first victim's house, she had felt pulled in a particular direction. She believed it was the route the rapist had followed after his crime. Because of the late hour, they tried to follow the pull in the car, but Nancy quickly lost it.

She had better luck after visits to other victims' homes. The meetings produced no new information but confirmed the impressions she had gotten from the first victim—the one who so closely resembled her. The interviews also confirmed another fact that Nancy found frightening—that she was indeed the type of woman who appealed to the man they were hunting. That made her wary.

After each interview she would stare down at the sidewalk and allow herself to be drawn by some invisible force that guided her like radar. Viewed by passersby, the scene caused some amusement—a tall, attractive woman tilted forward, peddling along the sidewalk at a brisk clip, her head cocked down and two suited gentlemen hustling to keep up with her.

Just before stepping down from the curb at one intersection, Nancy felt a strong hand grab her arm and jerk her violently back. It broke the trance, but she was pleased to see, as a speeding car brushed past, that the officer had saved her life.

Each of these forays wound through the streets of West Wilmington in circuitous, seemingly random patterns, but they always brought Nancy back to a large mailbox at one particular street corner. After the unlikely coincidence occurred for the second time, it dawned on Nancy that perhaps the rapist lived on one of the nearby streets. She looked up at the street signs and the name Shallcross Avenue caught her attention.

"He lives on this street," she said. "No. He stays here, but he doesn't live here permanently. He comes and goes."

The two officers who replaced Jay and Leroy for the day and who had never worked with Nancy before were understandably put off by her bold statement; they looked at her with heads cocked and smiles tugging at the edges of their mouths.

"Oh?" said one.

"Exactly which house?" asked the other, interested to see how far Nancy was willing to go.

Nancy surveyed the street. "I can't be sure."

The smiles became more obvious.

"Let's go. It's not safe," Nancy said.

The officers did not argue. They felt foolish enough chasing after this housewife and had no intention of annoucing to their sergeant that the civilian had taken them to the street where the rapist lived. Nancy, who was painfully aware of their feeling toward her, had an easier time handling that than her growing sense that their rapist was at that moment watching them. She knew this was a man capable of much more than rape and had no desire to confront him, even with two armed police officers.

Nancy was pleased when Jay and Leroy showed up the next day.

At yet another victim's residence, Nancy was again struck by the woman's resemblance to her. She had the same hair color, body build, and approximate height. She greeted the detectives warmly but seemed overcourteous in her nervousness, then led them down a narrow hallway. At the point in the hallway where a door led downstairs, Nancy was shaken with a sudden chill.

It was noticeable enough for the woman to stop and say to Nancy, "That's where he was standing, waiting for me with the ax."

"I had just gone to the bus stop with my daughter and had come back and was going to do laundry. He was standing there. He described my daughter, said how vulnerable she was and how beautiful she was and that if I gave him any trouble..." She began to cry.

"You don't have to go on. I understand," Nancy said.

"No," the woman said. "It helps."

And so she related the day's events to Nancy as they walked into the kitchen and she seated her visitors at the table. She asked if anyone wanted coffee. Nancy could feel that Jay and Leroy were ready to say no when both saw the same disappointment in her face and changed their order. She relaxed immediately. Somehow she needed the normalcy of serving them coffee.

When they were leaving, the woman grasped Nancy's hand and said to her, "You know we loved this house and we've lived here ten years, but now we're going to sell it. I can't feel safe here anymore. And my daughter..."

Nancy nodded and patted her hand. "I understand," she said.

Even the brilliance of the morning sun in its cloudless sky could not burn away the sadness they all felt that day. Nancy started her tracking routine almost immediately. And again, she ended up at the familiar mailbox facing Shallcross.

This is ridiculous, she said to herself. *We're in plain sight of the house here. I might as well go up there.*

"Are you guys wearing sidearms?" she asked. The two detectives looked at each other with puzzled smiles and then pulled their jackets back discreetly to reveal their shoulder holsters.

"Yes ma'am," they said in unison.

Nancy nodded approvingly, pulled herself upright, and started marching willfully up the middle of Shallcross. She moved so quickly that Jay and Leroy had to trot after her to catch up and almost stumbled when, only a short way up, she stopped abruptly. She looked pointedly at a two-story brick home with a wooden porch and said with assurance, "That one." Immediately she started her march back to the mailbox.

Leroy hustled back with their civilian while Jay stayed to jot down the number. It was 1002.

Back at the mailbox, Jay told Nancy that they had already been checking out the people on the street and he wasn't sure, but he thought 1002 was the home of a minister.

"He doesn't regularly live there. He visits there," Nancy said. "They have no idea what they've got on their hands, no idea what he's doing. They think he's their friend."

They'd be back and have a talk with him, Leroy said, but now they were going to get Nancy home.

In the end the talk wasn't necessary. Although no one knew it at the time, a critical piece of evidence had been discovered at the scene of the most recent rape, the attack in which the rapist had asked to use the phone book. In handling the book, he had left clear prints. Det. Jack Sines, the chief investigator on the case, immediately transported the book personally to the FBI lab in Philadelphia for analysis.

The result was almost instantaneous. The book contained prints so distinctive that it took only a short time to trace them to Aubrey McKay, thirty, an inmate at the Delaware Correctional Center at Smyrna who was serving a thirty-year sentence for manslaughter. When police checked the computer, they learned that McKay had been on a work release furlough from Smyrna each time one of the attacks in Wilmington occurred.

McKay was a violent criminal whose lengthy prison term stemmed from the shooting death in February 1969 of a retired, crippled gardener in Westover Hills. The man was killed when he surprised three men burglarizing his home. McKay was one of the men.

Before coming to Delaware, the FBI had sought McKay for a murder charge in Newark, New Jersey, and he was wanted by police in Union, New Jersey, for the alleged rape of a thirte-year-old.

In prison McKay received a high school diploma and took almost every education course offered at Smyrna. Leroy Landon, who along with Jay Ingraham was kicking himself for not recognizing Nancy's description of the Smyrna prison uniform, recalled their mistaken impression of Nancy's comment that he was taking college courses. Larry took a picture of McKay around to the victims and all identified him as their attacker.

The subsequent investigation revealed that McKay's furloughs were not being monitored according to regulations. When he was released, he was officially transferred into the custody of a prison guard. But McKay was actually spending his furloughed time living with his girlfriend in Wilmington. She was the daughter of a Baptist minister and still lived at home. Her address was 1002 Shallcross Avenue.

Ten

While the First Snow
Is Still on the Ground

By the time of Heidi's eye operation in August
the Spahn investigation had ground pretty much to a halt. Dutton
was being prosecuted for possession of stolen property and
weapons violations, but without a body, an indictment in the
Spahn disappearance was pointless.

The eye surgery, as unnerving as it seemed, went off without a
hitch, but not without some suspense when no one thought to tell
Nancy and John when it was over. Heidi, exhausted from an
anxious and sleepless night before, snoozed for four hours in
recovery while Nancy and John stewed, certain something had
gone wrong.

When the elevator doors finally opened and the full-sized
gurney carrying a tiny, rumpled Heidi at one end emerged, they
were both beside themselves. Heidi lay curled in a ball, her pacifier
wobbling in her mouth. She was dusting the end of her nose with

her favorite diaper and scanning the hallway anxiously for something familiar. Her head would not stop swiveling, as she voraciously drank in her surroundings. It was as if she were seeing for the first time. At close range Nancy was stunned at how little sign there was that an operation had even occurred. The eyes were a little bloodshot on the sides but perfectly centered. The difference in the baby's appearance was stunning.

Heidi scanned face after face as she searched for something safe and familiar. When her gaze passed over Nancy it was without recognition. The snub was so painful, Nancy cried out in protest.

"Heidi!"

No sooner was the word out than Heidi's little head snapped around and her eyes locked on to Nancy like a missile-tracking system. Then she launched, springing onto Nancy's chest so fast that their foreheads smacked. Heidi grabbed chunks of Nancy's long hair in her little fists and Nancy clutched tight her baby's trembling body.

Life for the Andersons was never uneventful, but crises the magnitude of Heidi's late arrival, her seizures, and the eye surgery seemed to subside as fall arrived. Travis entered first grade and revealed that he was profoundly color-blind. A teacher noticed that while on some days his coloring by numbers was accurate, on other days it was completely wrong. Questioned, Travis explained that sometimes he could get a classmate to arrange his crayons numerically, otherwise he just guessed at the right crayons, most of which he couldn't differentiate.

The fall also brought two new and frustrating police cases. Following on her uncanny accuracy in the Aubrey McKay case, the Wilmington police once again enlisted Nancy's help, this time in the brutal murder of Charles Deaner. Deaner had been tied to his bed and beaten to death. Nancy provided a description of the assailant that included the type of jobs he had held. Her information matched a suspect already identified by police; however, their investigation never developed enough evidence to prosecute.

In November Nancy was asked to help find the six-year-old daughter of a Wilkinsburg, Pennsylvania, police officer. Beth Lynn Barr had disappeared while walking home from school one afternoon in the usually quiet Pittsburgh suburb. Witnesses, who were later hypnotized in an effort to enhance their memory of the incident, recalled only that they had seen the first-grader enter the car of a man with sunglasses.

Nancy said from the outset that the girl was dead and that her body would not be found "until the spring thaw." She also provided details of the car used in the abduction, a physical description of the abductor, and a play-by-play of the events leading to the child's death. In addition Nancy told police the man had committed other abductions in western Pennsylvania. She provided enough details that police were able to match them with several open cases. A police artist with whom Nancy worked said he recognized the face she was describing from the description provided by a child who had survived one of the other abductions. The skeletal remains of Beth Lynn Barr were found in March of 1979—sixteen months after her murder, during the spring thaw, as Nancy had predicted.

Despite the detailed information she provided, the Barr case was never solved. Local police later would say that nothing Nancy told them was of any help.

Early in 1977 Nancy had been contacted by a freelance reporter from the Philadelphia area who thought an article on Nancy's police work would be of interest to the *National Enquirer*. In addition to stories about the private lives of celebrities, the Florida-based tabloid's editorial mix also included stories about psychics and the paranormal. So enthralled were its readers with the subject that the *Enquirer* kept on retainer a stable of psychics who received an annual salary to make predictions for the paper only.

Nancy was a natural. She was an attractive housewife from Newark, Delaware, helping good guys catch bad guys through use of her unusual paranormal powers. Moreover, a raft of Delaware

State Police officers, from Williams to the superintendent, were willing to go on the record attesting to her usefulness.

When the seventeen-inch article finally appeared on November 29, it contained numerous errors. But Nancy found herself in good company. The front-page teaser for her article was sandwiched between headlines that promised to tell the reason Steve McQueen and Ali MacGraw split up and the details of George Peppard's "Recent Brush With Death." Nancy's teaser was headlined, "Psychic Housewife Helps Police Solve Murder."

The article itself appeared on page thirty, and reported generally and erroneously on the Mary Allen case. In the article Williams and Smith were lavish in their confirmation of Nancy's abilities and usefulness. Although both were quite willing to confirm Nancy's abilities, they said they had been misquoted. Ten un-named investigations were referred to, in addition to the search for Zandy Bisson and Nancy's uncanny handicapping of the now-famous HAPS race at Brandywine Park.

The one article made Nancy an overnight celebrity nationwide with the *Enquirer*'s millions of readers, and for a brief time, her workload increased dramatically as new cases from across the country poured into her office.

As a result of the story, Nancy was invited to participate in the *Enquirer*'s psychic squad. Although the money from the *Enquirer* and the extra work would have helped the young family's tight budget, Nancy decided to decline. The misquotes and errors in the article and the trouble it had caused Colonel Smith and Sergeant Williams convinced her that regularly appearing in the tabloid could jeopardize her credibility and her ability to help the police. Her work was worth more than instant celebrity.

Among the out-of-state cases Nancy worked as a result of the *Enquirer* article was a murder that had horrified residents in Winchester, Virginia. A fifteen-year-old girl from nearby Front Royal had been abducted from a local shopping center and was missing. Sheriff Carroll K. Mauck and his deputy, Robert L. Edmundson, decided to call Nancy when their own investigation seemed stymied. They drove the three and a half hours from Winchester and arrived in the evening, armed with maps, a photo lineup of suspects, and items important to the victim. Nancy proceeded to draw a map of the parking lot where the abduction took place, accurately placing such details as a dumpster, gas pumps, and a grocery store. She went on to describe the car used in the abduction and the location of the girl's body. Nancy told the pair she heard a lot of traffic, sensed water nearby, and could smell something like burning rubber.

Mauck and Edmundson later found the body in a cornfield less than a quarter mile from a busy interstate highway, fifty yards from a pond, in a spot where the cool air of evening brought with it the pungent smoke from a brake manufacturer not far away.

From the photo lineup, Nancy unknowingly picked their prime suspect.

The arrival of the new year put Nancy's reading on Susie Spahn on the line. For fourteen months she had held to her belief that Susie Spahn's remains would be found while the first snow of 1978 was still on the ground. Since late 1976 she had had to defend it many times as Carl and his impatient squad members went scrambling after a variety of alternate interpretations.

All day long on New Year's Day 1978, as she moved about keeping the children occupied and preparing a ham, Nancy found herself frequently and reflexively casting an inquiring eye out the window toward a cloudy and threatening sky. The temperature hovered around the freezing mark and the air felt like snow.

Carolyn and Paulette Dawson also kept their eye on the gray sky as with another couple they worked their way through the eleventh green at the Hercules Country Club just north of Wilmington. The two sisters were avid golfers, fond enough of the game to come out on a freezing Sunday in January for a holiday round. At first they were merely distracted by the dog they saw playing with what looked from a distance to be an odd-shaped ball. But as they walked up the fairway, the two nurses saw that it was not a ball but had a familiar and unnerving shape to it. Paulette distracted the dog by throwing a stick, while Carol walked closer to what she could now see was a human skull. Retrieving another twig from the edge of the fairway, she lifted the skull up and placed it in a trash receptacle to keep it safe from animals. The foursome debated what to do as they played one more hole, then decided to call police.

That afternoon, as the boys played, Heidi slept, and John worked in his basement office, Nancy finished cleaning up the kitchen from their holiday meal. She had just settled in to see if there was anything besides college football on television when the phone rang. It was Hawkinson.

"Is this the one?" he asked.

"Who is this?"

"Oh," he said. "I'm sorry, Nance, but it's snowing and I wanted to be sure this was the one."

"Hawk?" Nancy said. She looked once more out the window. "Well, it's not snowing here." There was a long pause.

"Oh." He sounded disappointed.

"I don't know," Nancy said. "Maybe." They would just have to wait and see. Nancy hung up, newly worried over whether her prediction would be accurate. She had not been off the phone more than five minutes when another member of the old unit reported in that snow had begun to fall outside his house in Wilmington.

Nancy again checked outside her own house. The sky remained overcast, but so far it had not begun to snow. Though Carl's unit had been broken up and its members reassigned, within the next half hour detective after detective from the original investigation checked in. The sequence of their calls tracked the progress of the storm as neatly as any radar.

The Williamses, who lived furthest south of Wilmington and closest to Newark and Nancy, were the last to call.

"It's snowing, Nancy," Kitty said.

"It's not snowing where I am," she said.

Kitty relayed her message to Carl.

From behind Kitty in muffled tones she could hear, "Well, it better damn well start snowing where Nancy is, because I'm sick of waiting for Susie to be found."

Nancy hung up the phone and suddenly noticed tiny, widely spaced flakes drifting leisurely down to lie on the brown grass. A smile spread across her face as she considered even nature's seeming obedience to Carl's blustering commands. She found the sight of the falling flakes to be hypnotizing. Soon all doubt evaporated as a profound sense of peace flowed through her. She suddenly knew Susie would be found just as she had said.

When the phone rang again, she knew it was Mrs. Spahn.

"It's time, isn't it?" Susie's mother said.

"Yes, I feel it is, " Nancy replied. "A lot of other people think so too. Just about everybody on the old unit has called this afternoon to tell me it was snowing."

There was relief and gratitude in Mrs. Spahn's voice. "I thought they had given up," she said.

"Not these guys," Nancy said. "You can bet come morning they're going to be out driving around the area I described, trying to find her."

"And they *will* find her?"

"She'll be found now, yes, " Nancy said. "I feel sure of it."

"I want to find her and I don't want to find her."

"I can certainly understand that," Nancy said. "I'd feel the same way. But it would be nice to know if all those sightings were real or not and to resolve this in your own mind."

There was a long pause, then Mrs. Spahn said, "I know she's gone because she never would have done this to me."

When his squad had been split up, Carl had been assigned with Sacco to internal investigations within the attorney general's office. Hawkinson, Meyer, and Patterson had also been reassigned, so squad members did not immediately know about the skull that was at that moment being matched against persons recorded as missing during the past two years.

But Nancy did. Irvin Smith had called her shortly after the report of the skull got to him and asked if she thought it was Susie. Would she, he asked, be willing to join the search for the body once the identity was nailed down? At first Nancy didn't see the usefulness of her being present, but when Smith reminded her that she had emphasized the importance of evidence they would find at the site, she agreed to help.

It was not until late Wednesday that dental records confirmed that the skull was indeed Susie. Colonel Smith ordered a massive search of the woods around the twelfth green at Hercules, utilizing recruits from the state police academy. The search was scheduled for Thursday morning.

Hawkinson, who was working in the same office as Sacco, was the first to get the call. When Sacco arrived, Hawk jumped to his feet and grabbed his coat before Sacco had time to sit down.

"They think they've found Susie, " he said.

Nancy was instantly on both of their minds as they walked briskly out to the parking lot and piled into Sacco's car.

The January sky was overcast, but already the two detectives could tell the weather forecast, which called for a high of forty-one, was probably going to be on the mark. If the mercury climbed that high, this would be the warmest day of the New Year—the first to get above freezing—and assure that the fragile inch of snow that had fallen January 1 would be completely gone by noon. Even as it was, the snow had survived only in patches of shade.

"The last of the first snow," Sacco observed.

"She scares the hell out of me," said Hawk recognizing the quote from Nancy's reading more than fourteen months ago.

Hawkinson had never been comfortable around Nancy, but not because he was a skeptic. Just the opposite. His fear was that one day she would look squarely at him and see something awful in his future.

"What did she say?" Sacco began to recall. "Brandywine, hilly, large rocks, a lot of undergrowth, trees, and a river nearby. The word *Brandywine*. Motors. She said she heard little motors in the background."

"Golf carts," offered Hawkinson as Sacco turned onto Lancaster Pike, a two-lane road that ran along one side of the Hercules Golf Course.

"A nature preserve and a well-manicured lawn," Sacco continued. "Hercules doesn't exactly allow hunting along the fairways. I don't know why we didn't think of it," said Hawkinson.

"Does this road cross a river?"

"Red Clay Creek down here," Hawkinson said, pointing toward a bend in the road.

"And Brandywine Springs Park. That's within a few miles, isn't it?"

"Two or three," Hawkinson said.

Sacco looked out his window toward a thick stand of trees that bordered the golf course and casually said for no particular reason, "There. I'll bet that's where he dumped her."

And it was. But it would take another hour for the search team to find her.

After dropping Hawk off, Sacco went to get Nancy. Pulling into a maintenance road, the pair wound their way to the twelfth green, where Sacco parked next to a growing throng of police officers, golf course workers, and what seemed like a handful of disappointed golfers. A few reporters with notepads and photographers were also poking around the scene. The body had not yet been found and a police line had not yet been established.

Although Nancy's role and her prediction in the Spahn case had been kept out of the press, they were well-known among police officers. Quite a few cops from surrounding jurisdictions had found their way to the Hercules Country Club that morning personally to assess the accuracy of Nancy's prediction. Some had worked with her before and smiled or nodded as they passed, walking up the steep hill and into the thick trees where the search was concentrated. Others made a point of giving her a wide berth.

Nancy noticed that many were wandering into the search area carrying coffee cups and smoking cigarettes—items that could contaminate the site. Certain that two tiny pieces of evidence crucial to the case were somewhere in these woods, she began reminding officers that they were entering a search area. Some thanked her for the reminder; others were less gracious, glaring at her as she collected their cups.

Without the sun, the morning air and frozen ground chilled Nancy and she found herself bouncing from one foot to the other to keep warm. Sacco would stand with her for a while, then walk the twenty or so feet to the search area, where recruits on their hands and knees inched their way over the icy forest floor.

Nancy, however, had a sense that the need for a detailed search for evidence wasn't being taken seriously, so when Sacco returned from one of his sorties, she reminded him. "Remember what I said about the physical evidence. There are two pieces that will be crucial to making your case, but they could be easily overlooked. Without them you'll never link the murderer to Susie."

Sacco nodded, though he knew his encouraging a more thorough search would not go down well with the officer in charge. But like Nancy, he was fixed on closing this case.

Steeling himself for the inevitable rebuke, he marched over and announced in as diplomatic a manner as he could, "I just want to remind you that when I brought Nancy down on a search in Brandywine Park last year, she was adamant that we were going to find something near the body that would link the victim with her killer."

"No shit," came the annoyed reply. "You always find something around the body."

Sacco knew that wasn't true, but he didn't argue.

"What do you think, we're stupid?"

Sacco didn't reply.

The discovery of the main portion of the body came at 11 A.M., about two hours after the search had started. The first sign Nancy had was excited voices coming from the dense woods directly in front of her. Around her, officers sipping coffee and talking quietly among themselves heard it too. They dumped their cups and hurried into the trees.

Nancy's impulse was to move in exactly the opposite direction—away from what she knew they had found. But she stayed, feeling suddenly very alone. Sacco, who had been in the trees when the excitement started, walked over and confirmed that they had found some bones.

Sacco returned to the search and those left behind strained to see through the thick branches, where only movement and the patches of surviving white snow could be discerned.

Orders were now being barked as additional bones were found and the searchers closed in on the spot Sacco had so cavalierly pointed to from Lancaster Pike. Several men suddenly trotted from the search area toward a waiting ambulance that was parked behind Nancy. A moment later they walked back up with a gurney with retractable legs.

Almost at the same instant the sun burst out from behind the clouds that had been obscuring it all morning. There was a noticeable warming of the air as Nancy watched with amazement the discovery of Susie's body and the simultaneous melting of the last of the first snow of the year. The words of her own prediction chilled her. It had its effect on others as well.

One by one the police officers who were gathered in little knots that dotted the hillside looked down at Nancy, and then back into the thick of the forest, where the search continued. Then they grew silent and slowly moved away into the woods, out of Nancy's line of sight. The effect on Nancy was devastating. Already frightened by her own uncanny accuracy, she now felt even further isolated. She leaned against a nearby tree and prayed to God for Susie's family—and maybe, in a way, for herself.

For the next fifteen minutes or so the thicket was crowded with searchers, who seemed to fan out from a spot among the trees, working their way toward Nancy and the police line in one direction, Lancaster Pike in the other.

And then abruptly, it seemed to Nancy, it was over. The two men with the gurney walked slowly down the hill toward the ambulance. Between them was a blanket covering a raised mound about the size of a small person. A moment later the forest seemed to disgorge its human contents. Dozens of police officers walked out of the woods and down the hill, buzzing with conversation. As they approached Nancy, they began moving to her left or right, well before nearing the tape. By the time they arrived at the tape, not one was within twenty feet. Even officers she knew avoided eye contact. Even Hawk made a wide circle and left the scene with another officer.

Nancy had grown used to the uneasiness that many people, especially police officers, experienced around her. Usually it dissipated as they got to know her, but today it persisted like the lingering chill.

Even Sacco, who was among the last to emerge from the trees, seemed a little reserved when he got back to the police line and confirmed for Nancy that they had found the body and that there had been three large rocks nearby—rocks with the initials painted on them just as she had described.

"I don't know why we didn't think of this place, " Greg said.

"Did they find the evidence?" Nancy asked.

Sacco smiled. "Tiny little pieces of plastic about the size of a matchbook. Ragged along one edge. Two of them. And a wire."

She and Sacco returned to his car and wound their way out the access road and onto Lancaster Pike. As they drove past the cluster of trees where Susie's body had been found, Sacco pointed to it and said, "Just clowning around this morning, I pointed down there and told Hawk that's where he dumped her."

"I keep telling you guys you've got it too."

Sacco nodded.

With the discovery of the body, police began making their case against Dutton. Only days before the search at Hercules, Dutton, who had been in the Delaware Correctional Center near Smyrna since his arrest August 3, was sentenced to three years based on his plea of guilty to possession of a deadly weapon, receiving stolen property, and possession of marijuana.

In February a frustrated Irvin Smith called on Nancy to help identify a woman who had washed up on Slaughter Beach along the Delaware River. Police had sought the woman's identity for almost a month before turning to Nancy.

The call to Nancy set in motion an unlikely sequence of events that resulted in a positive identification being made within days. Smith had authorized his public information officer, Capt. Gerald R. Pepper, to solicit Nancy's assistance. He was so impressed with her work that after the body was found, he issued a press release stating not only that Nancy's advice had led directly to the woman being identified, but that information she had provided over the telephone utilizing only the name Jane Doe and the date and location the body was discovered proved more accurate than conclusions drawn by the medical examiner.

One of the errors made by the ME's office was the length of time the body had been in the water. The medical examiner originally estimated one to four days, while Nancy estimated two weeks or longer. Though the medical examiner later revised his estimate to one to two weeks, the victim had actually jumped from the Delaware Memorial Bridge December 12. She had been found January 21. Not only did this error incorrectly restrict the field of missing persons, but it had a bearing on the extent of the deterioration of the body, which resulted in an inaccurate composite drawing.

That was another point Nancy made in her phone reading—that the family would not recognize the composite because it was not a true likeness. Among the mistakes was the color of the eyes. The medical examiner had said they were brown, which they had become after death. The victim's true eye color was blue. Nancy noted in her phone reading that "something about the eyes is wrong."

Based on Nancy's information and her comment that "the woman's identity would have to come from Salem, New Jersey,"

Captain Pepper contacted the Salem Police Department, which referred him to the New Jersey State Police. They contacted the Delaware Memorial Bridge Police who, when given the correct time frame, did in fact have a report of a missing woman that matched. Only their missing woman had blue eyes, not brown. A Newcastle County detective, who was a cousin of the missing woman, was asked to view the Jane Doe that had washed up on Slaughter Beach anyway. The victim turned out to be his cousin— Donna M. Marenco, twenty-one, of 13 Dunbar Road, Newark, Delaware.

Police laid out their case against Dutton to a Newcastle County grand jury in March. The grand jury indicted him for first-degree murder. Newspaper reports at the time said police characterized their evidence as "substantial." In all they would present over one hundred pieces of physical evidence and more than forty witnesses who would tie Dutton to key pieces of it. But as strong as their case was, it ultimately hinged on putting Dutton at the scene where the body was found. That could only be accomplished by the two matchbook-sized pieces of broken gun grips and the odd piece of wire that Nancy had foreseen in 1976. Still, police had only one witness to the murder, and Nancy was, as Carl had once called her, a silent witness. No jury would ever hear her version of events.

Dutton's trial was scheduled to begin September 26. Awaiting it kept everyone on edge throughout the summer of 1978. Police worked to tie up loose ends, and Nancy found her workload growing as word of her predictions in the Spahn case spread.

When the trial began, Nancy followed press reports closely to evaluate whether her vision of events would be corroborated by the testimony of witnesses. Among the witnesses was Dr. Ali Z. Hameli, Newcastle County's medical examiner. Nancy had said that after Spahn and Dutton argued, Dutton struck Susie in the jaw and later, outside the car, struck her repeatedly. Also, in Nancy's vision the murderer had strangled her with a wire, though it was Nancy's belief that by this time Susie was already dead. The presence of a wire at the scene was confirmed when one matching Nancy's description was found near the body. What Nancy had not seen was use of the young woman's bra, which was found wrapped around her neck.

Hameli's examination of the body determined that the cause of death was probably blunt blows to the face or neck. Those blows probably fractured a vertebra and may have severed an artery, causing massive bleeding. The victim, he testified, could have inhaled the blood and suffocated. However, he also said death could have been caused by strangulation from the bra found wrapped around her neck.

Dr. John Lawrence Angel, curator of physical anthropology at the Smithsonian Institution in Washington, to whom Hameli had sent Susie's remains for a second opinion, concluded that she had suffered a violent contact blow from under the jaw, probably while her mouth was open, which would be consistent with Nancy's vision of Susie being struck while she argued with Dutton. The broken vertebra, he said, was probably due to considerable localized pressure from something around the neck. He did not say whether it was the bra or the wire. However, an FBI agent who testified at the trial said the wire and a short wooden stick found at the scene could have been used to make a Spanish windlass, which is a device used to increase tension in a loop of cord or wire. Hameli acknowledged that if the wire that was found at the scene had been looped around Susie's neck and tightened, it could have caused the damage found in her neck vertebra.

Probably the most revealing insight into what actually happened that night came from a nineteen-year-old inmate from Smyrna who testified that Dutton had bragged to him that he had killed Susie when she rejected his sexual advances. Richard Page, who was being held without bail pending sentencing for burglary, said Dutton was high on marijuana one night and started talking about the murder. The following account of Page's testimony in the *News Journal* newspapers is strikingly similar to Nancy's vision:

Page said that Dutton told him that Miss Spahn, whom Dutton had met previously in a nightclub, had accompanied him outside to his car, where he had invited her to get high. Dutton said he tried to have sex with the girl but she refused and wanted to go back into the nightclub, Page said. But Dutton got mad and forced her to go with him.

Dutton was more or less bragging and "trying to impress" me, Page said.

Dutton said he then went somewhere and parked, and tried again to get fresh, to have sex with the girl, and again she refused. "He got real mad because he's not used to being turned down by women," Page testified.

Page said Dutton told him he tried to strangle Miss Spahn with a necklace, but it wouldn't work, so he used a piece of wire.

Two or three weeks later, Page said, Dutton told him how he disposed of the body. Dutton said he dragged the girl from the car near some bushes, but the ground was too hard there, according to Page. So he took her further into the woods and buried her as deep as he could dig with his hands.

The critical importance of the handle grips became clear about midway through the trial, when the prosecution presented evidence to show that a Colt pistol with grips matching the pieces found near Susie's body were among items stolen in the Maryland burglary for which Dutton had already pleaded guilty. Dutton's brother-in-law, Gordon W. Eaton, testified that on November 13, about a week after Susie's disappearance, Dutton showed him a .22 caliber pistol with a missing hammer spring and no grips and asked if he could get parts for it. When Eaton asked about what looked like blood on the weapon, Dutton told him that he had gotten into a fight outside a Newark bar and that he had left a man lying in a parking lot, not knowing if he was dead or alive.

Eaton, who was an electrical maintenance worker for the Du Pont Company, also identified a crimp connector on the piece of wire found with the body as the same type he had given Dutton.

The case went to the jury on November 2. The jury deliberated for five and a half hours before being dismissed. The length of their deliberation troubled the prosecutor. The next day they deliberated for six more hours before reporting back to the judge that they were hopelessly deadlocked. A mistrial was declared.

The prosecutor was so angry at the outcome that he punched a sign in the lobby and knocked it off its base. He called the result the most frustrating experience he had ever had as a lawyer.

A new trial date was set for January 17, 1979.

Eleven

New Beginnings, New Directions

By the time of the Spahn mistrial, certain parts of Nancy's life were beginning to fall into place. Her work now required a major portion of her day and sometimes necessitated her being gone overnight. She was teaching adult courses in meditation for the Delaware Technical and Community College three evenings a week. Requests for speeches at colleges throughout the East were beginning to trickle in and private readings were booked three months in advance.

Her police work was escalating. Although Irvin Smith had now retired, Leroy Landon had begun to play the role of Carl Williams on cases in the Wilmington police jurisdiction. He and Nancy became fast friends as her presence at "the hall," as Wilmington's police headquarters was known, became commonplace. At first Landon found himself greeted by the whistled theme from the *Twilight Zone* whenever he came to work, but it was not long before his arrival with Nancy was followed by the quick formation of a knot of officers lining up to bounce their cases off Leroy's new psychic sidekick.

In nearby Newcastle County, Det. Tommy Gordon, who later became commanding officer of the Newcastle County police, also used Nancy's talents. Ironically, Newark, her own community, never used Nancy "officially" because the chief remained a steadfast skeptic.

The feedback Nancy was getting from the officers with whom she worked told her that her visions and insight helped move their cases forward. As her experience grew, she found herself thinking more and more like a detective.

She had also become a popular speaker at community groups, where a standard part of her presentation consisted of doing capsule readings on willing audience members. Sometimes they wanted an answer to a personal question. Other times, working only from a name, she described them, the issues they were confronting, and how they might best deal with them. More than once her insight released a reservoir of dammed-up emotion and tears of relief poured out. Often these people would later tell Nancy that in that moment they felt closer to her than they had ever felt to anyone in their lives. These were among the most satisfying moments of her career—better in a deep and personal way even than seeing a murderer brought to justice.

Despite these moments, Nancy's sense of isolation grew. The friendly camaraderie of the police officers with whom she worked helped, but it had well-defined limits and she longed for personal closeness with others like herself.

The introspection that her burgeoning psychic skills had brought finally made her face how estranged she had grown from her husband. John, who had at first seemed fascinated by her opening now seemed to be spending more and more time at his campus office or, when he was home, in his basement office. In truth, as Nancy's notoriety grew, it placed new demands and pressures on a relationship that had been coasting for a long time.

As in most divorces, their physical separation occurred after many years of emotional emptiness. The adjustment had already been made in tiny increments over many months. Moving apart seemed almost anticlimactic, certainly more natural than the intimate loneliness they had both been sharing for so long. By the beginning of 1979 Nancy was essentially a single parent raising three children. She had moved the previous year to a five-bedroom house in a fashionable section of Newark, which she and her mother had purchased together and shared.

When the Spahn case again came to trial, she followed it closely in the papers and on television. But since the unit was dispersed, she only got occasional calls from former members. Carl and Kitty, however, remained close friends. She and Kitty breathed a sigh of relief when the second trial resulted in a conviction.

She had always found closure energizing. Certainly that had been true when she had finally resolved her doubts about her marriage. She assumed the new energy she felt came from chunks that had been tied up in ambivalence. Throughout the last years of the marriage, almost since opening, she had felt she was being required to stifle her abilities, to keep them in check in order to fit into the role of wife. Now she could give her undivided attention to the advice and guidance coming from deep within her. She was free to take her abilities as far as they would allow, but in what direction? In some ways she was in awe of the gifts she had been given, often wondering if she was using them in the right way or making the most of them. In matters like the divorce, she could rely on her inner guidance system to help her know what to do. But about the system itself, where was she to go for advice?

She prayed. She meditated. She watched for signs and listened for clear-cut instructions. Guidance in the past had come in all these ways. At the beginning there had been teachers who appeared to her psychically and who would provide her with information and lessons regarding her own growth. Occasionally they would return. But now she seemed to have reached a level where new teachers were needed, and either she was not wise enough to perceive them or they had yet to appear. For the time being anyway, she was on her own.

She read books on other psychics—Eileen Garrett, whom she admired for her honesty and clarity; *The Sleeping Prophet*, Jess Stearn's account of the psychic Edgar Cayce. Nancy had often wondered if there was any significance to her being born on the day Cayce died. Perhaps the book that hit closest to home was *The Reluctant Prophet,* given to her by her mother. In it Daniel Logan described his struggles as he wrestled with the spiritual commitment he was being asked to make.

Nancy well understood his dilemma. While people were willing, even eager to make use of prophets, they were also frightened by them. The Spahn case was a good example. Nancy's work had been so good that it created a degree of distance. It was as if her own success had hung a placard around her neck that said FREAK.

And yet she was quite sure God did not pick his teachers lightly. Though Nancy felt confident that she could turn her back on this part of herself and lightning would not strike her dead, she was equally sure that she would live the rest of her life with the sense that she had somehow let God down by failing to accomplish her reason for existence. She would lead her life with a sense of failure and mediocrity that she knew she could never tolerate. And so the question became, *How* was she to use it? Was the police work her life's work or was it just a training ground for something else?

Nancy asked for a sign. Then in June of 1979, she got a call from a detective from Anne Arundel County, Maryland, by the name of Jim Moore.

Detective Moore didn't have anything against psychics, he had just never seen them deliver. On the handful of occasions when they had been used by the department, they were unsuccessful in moving the case forward, and that for Moore was the bottom line. After all, active police investigations were not testing labs for the existence of paranormal phenomena. Information only mattered if it led to closure. And as far as he knew, information from psychics never had. At least not in any homicide cases he'd worked on.

He had a vivid memory of a tall, mysterious man dressed in black that the department had flown in from somewhere while Moore was still in uniform. Moore had been assigned to the scene that day after discovery of the body of a ten-year-old girl who had been literally butchered. It was the kind of case that required pulling out all the stops, and so the man in the flowing black overcoat was hauled to the scene. Moore watched as he walked the scene with detectives, interrogating them about everything they knew about the case. What seemed to be a critical piece of evidence was an old bowl which was partly filled with rainwater and what were believed to be traces of the girl's blood.

After extracting everything police were willing to share with him, the stranger went into a trance and returned with his "reading" on the case: the girl was the victim of a satanic cult; the bowl was used in the ritual that led up to her sacrifice. When the case was solved, the murderer turned out to be a little old man in the neighborhood who liked little girls. The rain-filled bowl was simply a convenient place to rinse the blood from his hands after he had killed her.

Moore's impression of psychics was formed.

Yet Moore, unlike some other cops, had never closed out the possibility that some psychic somewhere could be useful on some case. After all, he had heard detectives talk about Dorothy Allison, a psychic from Nutley, New Jersey, who had an excellent reputation for finding lost children. It was just that in his own experience he had yet to find one who had helped close a murder case.

It was that openness, however tentative, that would prove pivotal in solving one of the county's most perplexing homicides of 1979.

Detective Moore got the call late in the afternoon on June 8. Calvin S. Schilling, a local businessman who operated a successful septic tank cleaning firm, had returned from a business trip to Annapolis to find his wife's nearly lifeless body lying in a pool of blood in the living room of their modest house on Fort Smallwood Road in Riviera Beach. She had been stabbed eleven times.

Minutes before Schilling's arrival, at approximately 1:55 P.M.,

Mrs. Schilling had gotten off the phone with one of her children. Schilling arrived at about 2:30, so police knew with better than typical precision exactly when the murder had occurred.

What they did not know was why, although they quickly developed several working theories. One was that the killing had been directed at Schilling—either with the idea of robbery or revenge. Schilling's business, it was quickly learned, was successful partly because he employed low-paid, unskilled, transient workers. Many had criminal records and Schilling was not an easy man to work for. As is often the case with self-made men, he was outspoken, would take nothing from anyone, and feared little—including homicide investigators.

Between bouts of what seemed like genuine grief, he would berate the investigators with impatient belligerence, and yet he cooperated fully, submitting to hypnosis and polygraph tests. This contradictory behavior puzzled Moore, who was the lead investigator. Experience had shown him that guilty people behave in one of two ways: they either instantly demand to see a lawyer or try to become the investigator's best friend and ally in breaking the case. They even abandon their legal rights as they fix on convincing the authorities of their innocence. Schilling's response was a combination of the two, but other things inclined Moore to consider him a prime suspect. As the spouse, he was automatically a suspect; his alibi was soft and could be only generally confirmed; and he kept making odd comments like, "Well, if I did it, I don't remember doing it."

It was the comments that led to the hypnosis. But it was the man's outright hostility toward the investigators that kept him high on the suspect list. His case was not helped by the revelation that he was having an affair.

Moore's standard method of working a homicide was to begin by compiling a suspect list, then for each suspect to create columns of attributes that if confirmed would downgrade the likelihood of that particular suspect being guilty. The first column was alibi; if it was confirmed, the suspect would get a check mark. Other columns might be polygraph: the man would get a check if he passed; interview: a check mark if nothing questionable or incriminating was uncovered; gut feeling: a check mark if Moore's instincts told him the man was innocent. If a man got three check marks, Moore would begin focusing on someone else. This was usually an effective method of clearing suspects. But in the Schilling case, at the end of each sixteen-hour day he would look down over his list and inevitably find that he either had cleared no one or had added more suspects than he had cleared. He wasn't just treading water, he was sinking and he knew it. Three weeks into the investigation Moore looked at his list and saw that he had thirty-three suspects.

He sat down with his partner, Tommy Mott, to brainstorm. Both knew they were looking at months of methodical work to get through the suspect list—maybe as much as a year, because some of Schilling's transient workers would be difficult, if not impossible, to track down. They also knew that the likelihood of cracking a homicide declines rapidly with time, plummeting sharply after just the first seventy-two hours. Both agreed they needed something to expedite this case, but what?

Moore was uneasy about bringing in a psychic, but he decided if ever a psychic might be of use, this was the time. He refused to use any of the psychics the department had consulted in the past and decided instead to seek referrals from other departments, especially the nearby Montgomery County Police Department, for which he had considerable respect. In fact, his respect for their operation made him a little uneasy when he had to tell why he was calling. Moore was surprised when the lieutenant he spoke with not only didn't miss a beat, but seemed downright effusive in his description of a Newark housewife by the name of Nancy Anderson. Moore made other calls, collected other names, but no other reference was as strong as the one from Montgomery County.

When he made the call, he found himself surprised and oddly disappointed at the normalcy of the person on the other end.

"Now, what will you be needing?" he asked. "The case file?"

"Oh, God, no," Nancy said. "That will get in the way. Just bring a photo of the victim when she was alive. A photo of the victim at the scene. And a map."

"That's all?"

"That's what I need," Nancy said.

Suddenly Moore was again having doubts. This was too simple, too clean. She sounded like the lady next door. He weighed the recommendation of the Montgomery County Police Department against his own logic, which was telling him that this trip was going to be a waste of time. In the end, he decided it was unfair to prejudge this psychic for not living up to his stereotype.

He brought the case file anyway, on an impulse, and with it a manila folder with Xeroxed rap sheets and some mug shots of the suspects they had so far identified. He also brought slides of the murder scene and a carousel projector. What he did not have was a photo of Leonetta Schilling after the assault. The victim had been transported to the hospital before the police photographer arrived at the scene and autopsy photos were not yet available.

When Jim Moore, his sergeant, and Moore's partner arrived at Nancy's home that evening, there was certainly a degree of hopefulness among them, although it had only a thin edge over their doubts. The normalcy of Nancy's new home did little to encourage Moore. There were children arguing off somewhere in a bedroom and a dog sniffing at their feet. The faint smell of cooking struck him, though he couldn't identify the scent.

Nancy greeted the trio and, after hasty introductions and some background on each of the officers, found a spot near an outlet for Moore's projector. He had planned to project onto a wall but Nancy quickly retrieved a screen from the basement and set it up. When she returned, Moore had just about given up on his expectation of being led back to a dark room with a crystal ball. Nancy sealed it when she plopped down in her brown rocker and asked how she could help.

Again, his instinct was to walk out. This was all too casual.

"Well, we have a case that's giving us some trouble," he began.

"We have a woman, Leonetta Schilling, who was murdered in her living room in broad daylight. It has a lot of people scared. Frankly, we don't know what we're dealing with but we have a lot of suspects and no way to narrow them down."

Nancy nodded. "Did you bring the photos?"

"Oh, we don't have a photo of the victim after the assault, but we have shots of the scene—the slides. And I got these from her family." He reached across the small room and handed Nancy several photos of Leonetta Schilling at family events. She was a handsome older woman who seemed to Nancy unusually self-possessed. The quality that stood out was motherliness. She loved children.

Nancy leaned forward on the couch and rubbed her hand over the photo of the woman. When she was finished, she asked to see the slides of the crime scene. Visually, they were not very interesting, but from them events surrounding the day they were taken began to form in Nancy's mind. Next she psychometrized the map.

When she was finished, she put the objects down, cocked her head to one side, and began to tell the story of what happened to Leonetta Schilling on the last day of her life.

Because the victim was not pictured, Nancy expected the emotional intensity of the images to be lessened, so she opened herself more than usual. That turned out to be a mistake. When the images came, they were powerful.

"*Leonetta smiling and greeting someone. She hugs him. It is brief, informal, and yet there is an uneasiness within her because she senses that this person is going to ask her for money. This puts her into conflict because she has just had an argument with her husband over giving this person money. He says the person is no good and that she is not to give him any more money.*

"*She moves around, and they walk into the kitchen. She's moving because she's uncomfortable. This is partly because she's worried about him asking for money and partly because he seems edgy and this is adding to her nervousness. His thought pattern is very*

disturbed, characteristic of a mixture of drugs and alcohol, which
is weakening his self-control, making him irritable.

"They're chatting. I'm getting vignettes of the two sitting across
the same table at lunch, only they are much younger. He's wrapped in
an afghan and she's tucking him in on a couch. Very gentle with him.
The love in this woman is exceptional. He's in bed, she's reading to
him."

"Mother? No. More distant, but she has motherly feelings about
him. There is a bond, but it's not the same as a mother bond. But it is
familial.

"The side images are fading. We're back in the Schilling kitchen.
He is asking her for money. He does this in a petulant and demanding
way, as if he's owed it. His manner hits Leonetta the wrong way. She
is already nervous, a little frightened about a confrontation, and that
seems actually to push her into this uncharacteristic, assertive frame
of mind.

"She explodes in the way mothers sometimes do when they lose
patience with a difficult child. She kind of jumps him emotionally.
Her response seems to surprise even her. It escalates. She berates him
for his irresponsibility, the damage he is doing to his parents. She
knows where to hit; it's clear she knows him.

"He's badly hurt. Hearing how this woman truly sees him is
intolerable. He knows she's right and he can't face that. She's making
him deal with something that somehow he knows will destroy him.
This woman was very important to him and now he feels she no
longer values him. He has nowhere to go, nothing to throw back,
except threats. He tells her to shut up and feels a little better. Then,
sensing her fear, he begins to threaten her. It feels good to him to see
her frightened. To see her backing off. To be back in control. She tries
reasoning with him, but somehow everything she says seems to fuel
his rage.

"He takes a knife. At first it's a prop to threaten her. Then it's
reflexive. He plunges it into her and he feels the threat diminish.
With each blow he becomes bigger, more powerful, more right. And
she becomes smaller and less important. This brings blow after blow.

He can't stop.

"She is stunned at the change in him and can't react very well. She gets a hand up once or twice, but she is really paralyzed by his behavior. It is unreal to her. She can't process it until it is too late.

"He goes out the door. Bloody, oddly relieved, exhilarated. He's being watched and knows it. He runs to the back of the house, where he gets into a pickup truck and tries to explain what happened to the person behind the wheel. He's a young man too. He's shocked. One minute he's reading the paper and the next minute he's got this rambling, bloody man next to him talking in fits and starts. He's thinking, What kind of trouble is this guy in now and how much of it is going to rub off on me? But he's no fool. He sees that this person is out of control and dangerous. He asks a few questions and they leave the area."

Nancy opened her eyes to confront three staring faces. "I would say she knew him," Nancy said. "In fact, it appears that she baby-sat for him as a child."

"What about the witness?" Moore asked. "You said somebody was watching him when he came out of the house."

Nancy closed her eyes and returned to the scene. She saw an older woman watching from a nearby house and felt the woman not only knew Leonetta but recognized her killer. She described the woman as best she could. This time when she opened her eyes, the officers were nodding.

"Do you know who I'm talking about?" she asked.

Moore said that he believed they did. They had talked to an older woman not far from the Schilling house, but she had denied seeing anything.

Nancy asked for the map and pointed roughly to where she felt the witness's house was. "White stucco, I think," she said.

Moore scribbled some notes.

"Can you tell us anything more about the assailant?"

"He keeps changing jobs," she began. "The guy in the truck is someone he works with and they both have drug and alcohol problems. They're working some kind of construction right now, but

it's not skilled construction work, it's menial. That's about all I can get on him."

"It sounds like you really got a good look at the murderer. Were you actually watching him kill her?"

"Yes," Nancy said.

"If I showed you these mug shots and the killer's mug shot was among them, would you be able to identify him?"

Nancy looked mildly surprised. "Maybe," she replied. "I mean, you would think so, wouldn't you?"

The three men nodded hopefully.

Moore dug out his suspect file and handed it to her. Nancy thumbed through the rap sheets and assorted mug shots, ranging the photos and psychometrizing the signatures on the rap sheets. About two-thirds of the way through she suddenly fixed on a photograph. The thought pattern was familiar. She looked at it more closely. It was very similar to the thought pattern of the assailant.

She took the photo and attached sheet out of the folder and put it aside but found herself oddly distracted by it. Continuing through the folder, she was drawn again and again to the photo at her right, but she said nothing to the officers.

From the moment she had separated the photo from the pack, the officers had fixed on her, trying not to interrupt whatever processes were going on, but dying to know whom she had picked out. Finally, Moore could wait no longer.

"Why did you put that one aside?" he asked.

Her eyes locked on him briefly. "Because I think this is your perpetrator."

The three almost jumped for the sheet. Nancy turned it so that they could all see whom she had selected. The sergeant was the first to recognize the picture. He looked startled.

"Please don't tell me who it is until I finish the work and get through all of them," Nancy said.

But the work was even harder now. The officers were edgy and impatient and she found it hard to block out their rising excitement. She stiffened her concentration, fanned out the remaining sheets, and ticked them off one at a time.

Finished, she closed the folder and reached for the sheet on the suspect she had selected.

"This is so much like the thought pattern of the assailant that it's like an identical twin," she said. "The similarities are tremendous, but there are some differences. The man who killed Leonetta is in much worse shape with drugs than this man. But it feels so similar that I would have to say that this person needs to be checked into."

"That's her nephew, Allen Finke," Moore said, hardly containing his own excitement. "We put him on the list because he's had some problems, but in truth we haven't focused on him because everybody is telling us that they were very close. He's among our least likely suspects."

Once Nancy started talking, Moore had been grateful that he had put off contacting her until they had completed their groundwork. Otherwise, he would not have realized that almost everything she was saying fit information they had already confirmed about Finke through their own investigation. Most of it had never made the press.

"There's one problem with Finke, though," said Moore. "He has an airtight alibi. Worked that day. I saw the work records myself."

"Check again, and it would be a good idea to talk to the young man who drove him to the house."

"He does have a roommate," he said to his sergeant. "They work together for a home improvement company. Construction work."

"Wouldn't the guy who drove him to the scene be an accessory to murder since he hasn't come forward?" Nancy asked.

"That's what I'd call it," Moore agreed.

When they were finished, the officers shook Nancy's hand and thanked her. Moore paid her for the reading and they all piled into the car and headed back to Maryland. For a long time no one spoke. Finally the sergeant broke the ice. "We should have called that woman a month ago."

It was what they were all thinking and it opened the dam. From that moment on the excitement over what they had just witnessed came pouring out in animated conversation. It was as if they were talking about a baseball game filled with remarkable plays and new batting records.

The visit to Nancy was on Friday, July 6. On Monday morning Moore returned to Finke's place of work and arranged to talk to his boss. They had to break Finke's alibi or, despite Nancy's remarkable reading, there was no point in pursuing him further. Maybe, Moore thought, he had taken a late lunch that day, or a long lunch.

"Oh, that's easy to explain," Finke's boss said almost as soon as Moore had described their dilemma. "Allen Finke didn't work that day."

Moore looked at his partner, whose jaw was stuck slightly ajar.

"But I saw the work records for the day. He clearly worked," Moore argued.

"That's my fault," the man said. "See, I was picking him and his buddy up that morning in my truck and taking them out to the job. So I get there at 7 A.M. or so and bang on the door. Nobody comes, so I go in and they're crashed. I mean wrecked."

"So you leave?"

"Well, I said I'd wait while they got cleaned up, but when they dragged their asses out to the truck, they were too wrecked and I couldn't take a chance on them at the job. I told them to go back and sleep it off. I was late getting to the job by then, so I never got around to changing the work schedule."

The two detectives were stunned. Within forty-eight hours of Nancy's pointing them in the direction of one of their least likely suspects, his alibi was broken.

Next they focused on Finke's roommate.

For two full days they questioned the man, intermittently polygraphing him. He initially claimed that after the boss had left they slept until 11 or 11:30, then decided to get up and go out for more drugs. The dealer they used when they were tapped out for cash lived in Stony Creek, on Fort Smallwood Road just over the line from Riviera Beach. But on this day they were unsuccessful and returned home empty-handed. They spent the rest of the day at their apartment. End of story.

"You know," Moore said, "the only trouble with your story is that when we put you on the polygraph and ask whether you were at the Schilling house that day, you fail. How do you explain that?"

"It must be because we drove by the Schilling house on the way to our dealer," he said.

So the polygraph question was rephrased: "Other than riding by the Schilling house on Fort Smallwood Road, were you at the Schilling house that day?"

"No."

He failed.

On the second day, growing concerned that he was being placed at the scene of a murder, the roommate changed his story again.

"We get up eleven, eleven thirty, we decide to get some more drugs," he began. "We go over to the drug dealer in Stony Creek, but he isn't there or he wants cash or something. Anyway, we aren't successful. And we start back and Allen says, 'I know where we can get some money. My aunt and uncle are gone to Las Vegas on a gambling junket. There's nobody home. They always keep lots of money in the house—thousands of dollars. I'm going to break in and get us the money.'"

Moore felt excitement begin to stir within him. This story was ringing true. Moore already knew that the Schillings frequently went on gambling junkets and had been scheduled to go on one the day she was killed. This particular trip had been canceled, however, when the government grounded DC-10s following a crash in Chicago.

Finke's friend was now saying that he had pulled into a strip shopping center behind the Schilling home and parked. Finke had gotten out of the car, walked around the fence, and gone up to the back door. At that point, the friend said, he himself pulled out a newspaper and started to read and saw nothing else until Finke returned a few minutes later and said he had been unsuccessful at getting any money. They then drove home.

Moore was ecstatic. Thanks to a very important witness they had not known they had, they had now placed their prime suspect at the murder scene around the time of the murder.

Moore and his partner interviewed merchants in the strip plaza behind the Schilling house and found one retailer who remembered the friend's truck and corroborated much of his story. Within four days of visiting Nancy, Allen Finke was brought in for questioning.

If Moore had had any doubts about Finke, the man's own cooperation squelched them. From the first day they interviewed him through mid-week, when they talked well into the night, Moore periodically offered to take Finke home or let him leave on his own anytime he wanted. No, Finke would say, I want to convince you guys that I didn't do it. It was a classic response. Even though the investigators were inconveniencing the hell out of him and had talked to his friends and associates about the investigation, he remained friendly and cooperative. In Moore's experience, an innocent man would have long since become livid and challenged them in every legal way possible.

But not Finke. Although he kept failing the polygraph and bits and pieces of his story changed, his overall demeanor remained oddly friendly even as the truth began to emerge. After one round of questioning he finally conceded that he had in fact been to his aunt's house on the day of her murder but said that he had gone there to borrow, not steal money. He even recalled at one point seeing her lying on the floor dead but claimed he did not know how she had died.

Throughout it all Moore remained friendly and sympathetic, attentive to Finke's every need. Coke? Cigarette? Bathroom?

"Are you sure you don't want us to take you home?" he would say at least a dozen times during the last day of questioning.

"No, I want to prove to you guys that I'm innocent," Finke would reply.

Finally, when it had grown late and the investigators themselves were worn down, they asked if they could take him home or make a place for him to sleep there at the station. To their surprise he chose to stay. A meeting room was converted into a bedroom and Finke was put up for the night.

But Thursday morning when Moore arrived for work, Finke looked haggard and asked to be taken home. He no longer wanted to talk to investigators. Moore arranged transportation and then spent the day reviewing what they had. They did not have a confession, but they had one hell of a circumstantial case.

On Friday, one week to the day after their visit to Nancy, Glenn Allen Finke was arrested and charged with the murder of Leonetta Schilling. He was later convicted of first-degree murder and although a retrial was ordered because of a technical error in the original trial, he was convicted on the same charge a second time.

Today Jim Moore says that he doubts that the case would have been solved if they had not consulted Nancy.

It had been a textbook illustration of exactly how a psychic could be useful—even pivotal—in a police investigation. An enthusiastic police information officer was so impressed with Nancy's work that on his own authority he decided to announce Nancy's remarkable work to the world. He took the unprecedented step of turning out a press release documenting her reading and issuing it to all major media in the Baltimore area, along with the announcement of the arrest. The headline the next morning in the *Baltimore Sun*, one of the nation's ten largest newspapers, read: "Nephew Charged in Murder, Psychic Aids Schilling Probe." Not only did the main story give Nancy credit for cracking the case, but a sidebar detailed her work with Sergeant Moore.

While the notoriety didn't do the information officer's career any good, it made Nancy an instant celebrity. She suddenly found herself fielding calls and interviews from media throughout the East.

When the dust had settled a few days later, she found herself with one of those rare moments that mothers treasure. The boys

were gone to the neighborhood pool and Heidi was down for her
nap. Her mother was in her studio, painting. It was a brilliant July
day and Nancy relished the warmth of the sun on her skin as she
perched on the old picnic table that sat on the patio at the rear of
the house. July and August were her favorite months. They
reminded her of Chile and the wondrous days of her childhood.

A butterfly drifted into view. She felt an inexplicable sense of
calm flow through her as she watched its colorful wings work the
air. Someone had once described her as a butterfly with a
turboprop. She liked that. It seemed to capture the gossamer
quality of her inner life, her sensitivity and compassion, as well as
her appetite for life.

Released from the ambivalence of her marriage, the turboprop
now seemed to be revving up. Her thoughts were clearer, her work
reaching new levels of accuracy and detail.

She had asked for a sign and had been handed the Schilling case,
the most cut-and-dried success she had ever had. And now this
case, the best case she had ever worked, was making news. Was it a
coincidence? She didn't think so. She was no longer worried about
being labeled a freak. It was out of her hands. From this day
forward she would be defined by the Schilling case.

She allowed herself to be satisifed for a moment, even proud of
herself. And with that confidence came a new clarity of thought.
Maybe, she said to herself, the question was not whether she
should continue her police work, but rather what more she should
do as well with her special gift. She was just coming into her own.
Growth was the thing. Getting better and better, challenging
herself. Making the most of what God had given her in any way she
could. The public now knew her as a police psychic, maybe the
best there was. Schilling had made that clear. Now the question
was, what would come next?

Epilogue

Nancy's work continues. Since the 1970s she has gone on to work on cases as challenging and interesting as those described in *Silent Witness*. Many of these cases, however, are still pending, or legally unresolved, so it would be less than fair to discuss them here.

The events described in *Silent Witness* are so remarkable that even the most open-minded reader may wonder if there is any confirmation for their occurrence other than Nancy's recollection. Although I have tried to unobtrusively weave corroboration into the narrative, the reader is assured that Nancy's work on every major police case in this book was confirmed by at least one of the officers with whom she worked and in many instances several. Additional sources of confirmation included newspaper accounts and correspondence.

The conversations and thoughts contained in the book have been recreated based on interviews with Nancy and other witnesses to the conversations. No claim is made that these represent the exact words spoken almost two decades ago, but to the best of Nancy's recollection they capture the tone and represent the key information contained in those conversations.

In addition to corroborating information through interviews, some sections of the narrative were reviewed by officers familiar with the case being described. The section on Aubrey McKay was reviewed by Jack Sines, principal investigator on that case. Much of the Susie Spahn material was reviewed by Greg Sacco, as was the portion of the narrative dealing with Nancy's first day of police work—Jack White and the arson and her evolving relationship with Sacco and the Williamses.

Most of the officers described in the book have since retired. Carl Williams retired from the state police in 1982 and started Tri-Star Associates, a detective agency whose clients include some of the most prominent criminal attorneys in Wilmington. His departure from the state police corresponded to the time frame Nancy described the first day they met.

In 1992, Greg Sacco retired as a captain and commander of special investigation. He is currently supervisor of transportation for the Christina School District in Newark.

Irvin B. Smith retired from the state police in 1979 and served as U.S. Marshall for Delaware from 1979 to 1981. He later became chief of police for the city of Newcastle and in 1984 opened Eagle Investigators, Inc., a private detective agency.

Jim Moore retired from the Anne Arundle County Police Department in 1992 and is considering a second career as a writer. His subject: his most interesting police cases.

Jack White, through the heroic efforts of his family, especially his mother, regained consciousness though he has severely limited speech capabilities and is confined to a wheelchair. He lives with his mother in Bear, Dealware.

Bill Bonds returned home and graduated from Ohio University with a degree in accounting. A vice president with Helical Line Products, he is married and has two daughters, aged ten and twelve. They live in Bay Village on Lake Erie where during the summer Bill races sailboats almost every weekend.

Following the Schilling case, Nancy began receiving national attention. In the years since, she has become a popular guest on radio and television talk shows including "48 Hours," "Sightings," "Attitudes," "Geraldo Rivera," "Inside Story," "People are Talking," and "Evening Magazine." Profiles of her appeared in such national magazines as *Redbook*, *Woman's Day*, and *Women's World*. Her work was also featured in the books *Blue Sense*, *Who*

Killed My Daughter? and the Time-Life series *Mysteries of the Unknown.*

In 1981 Nancy moved to suburban Pittsburgh. She was married to Steve Czetli from 1982 to 1993. Together, they collaborated on many projects, including this book. Today she continues to mix public speaking, private readings, and police work from all over the country with the duties of a single parent.

Heidi, a high school honor student, discovered several years ago she had a talent for figure skating. She now competes nationally as well as locally in competitions organized by the Ice Skating Institute of America and the United States Figure Skating Association.

Travis's reticence evaporated during high school in the face of his six-foot-four frame and a sense of humor and style that made him popular with classmates. He graduated in 1992 and is a Territory Service Representative for the Keebler Co.

Blake found cooking allowed him to make messes in a socially acceptable way and received training as a cook.

George, Nancy's beagle, lived to a ripe old age. Today, George II, a beagle that looks a lot like him, is trying to fill his shoes.